"A 'must read' for the families I s   /ide
copies to their school nurses and administrators. I will also recommend
it to my colleagues in pediatrics and adolescent medicine. As a pediatrician, I find no greater pleasure than helping children grow and develop
into happy, healthy, well-adjusted adults. This resource will help me in
that goal for gender-variant and transgender youth."

      —Irene N. Sills, MD, Professor of Pediatrics, SUNY - Upstate
      Medical University, Joslin Center for Diabetes and Endocrinology

"Gracefully, sensitively, and thoroughly illuminates a topic that has been
shrouded far too long in fear and ignorance. Anyone who knows or
loves a transgender child must read this book."

      —Jamison Green, author of *Becoming a Visible Man*

"For far too long parents, families, friends, teachers and helping professionals have lacked a unified resource to help them navigate a reality that
can be perplexing and challenging. *The Transgender Child* provides tech-
nical information, supportive resources, and personal stories that will
positively impact the lives of transgender adolescents, children and their
families. It will play the role of a practical companion on a journey that
can be trying but also rewarding. The needs of transgender and gender-
variant youngsters and their families are multiple, complex, and varied.
Providing up-to-date and balanced information about a field of knowledge that is underdeveloped is not an easy task. With a clear commitment
to improve the lives of transgender children and their families, Stephanie
Brill and Rachel Pepper have achieved an inclusive and concise reading
that is a must have for all those involved."

      —Edgardo Menvielle, MD, Associate Professor of Psychiatry and
      Behavioral Sciences, The George Washington University, Director
      of the Gender and Sexuality Psychosocial Programs, Children's
      National Medical Center

"A great, practical guide that every parent should read. Parents, teachers, grandparents, and anyone who interacts with kids on a regular basis will find *The Transgender Child* to be a smart, accessible roadmap for what can often be an uncharted journey. Stephanie Brill and Rachel Pepper help parents cut to the chase so they can do what every parent does best: love and embrace their child, no matter who they are."

—Jody M. Huckaby, Executive Director of PFLAG

"This beautifully written, meticulously well-researched book is a godsend for parents and professionals in search of clear, reliable, and up-to-date information about all facets of parenting and caring for transgender children. Combining real-life experience with the latest research, Stephanie Brill and Rachel Pepper have written an indispensable guide that will save lives and empower families to ensure that transgender children receive the love and support they need to thrive."

—Shannon Price Minter, Legal Director, NCLR

The Transgender Child

Stephanie Brill and Rachel Pepper

CLEIS
PRESS

Published in the United States by Cleis Press Inc.

P.O. Box 14697

San Francisco, California 94114.

Printed in the United States.

Cover design: Scott Idleman

Text design: Karen Quigg

Logo art: Juana Alicia

10 9 8 7 6 5 4 3

Library of Congress Cataloging-in-Publication Data

Brill, Stephanie A.

The transgender child / Stephanie Brill and Rachel Pepper.

p. cm.

ISBN 978-1-57344-318-0 (pbk. : alk. paper)

1. Transgenderism. 2. Transgender youth. 3. Gender identity. 4. Transgender people. I. Pepper, Rachel. II. Title.

HQ77.9.B75 2008

306.76'8083—dc22

2008016481

Stephanie
For Aidan—my visionary playmate

Rachel
I dedicate this book to all the children who teach us about love and life every day, especially my own private tutor, Frances Ariel.

Table of Contents

Foreword

Autobiographical, sociological, and psychological books and novels about transgenderism abound. While the autobiographers often painfully recount their earliest gender discomfort, there is little evidence of their having received proper evaluation, counseling, or support. Early medical intervention is absent. Until the advent of the Internet, parents of transgender children were convinced that they were the only parents on the planet confronting the conundrum of gender identity variance in the face of their child's consistent genotypic, phenotypic, and biochemical sex.

When their gender-variant behavior became obvious to the immediate and extended family, neighbors, classmates, and school personnel, most children were subject to ridicule, verbal bullying, and physical abuse. Parents were advised to "redirect" their children's gender behavior or to restrict their access to the variant clothes and toys to a single room in the home and not to express atypical gender behavior elsewhere in word, dress, or behavior. Evidence for this approach is limited to just a few longitudinal studies claiming that less than 20 percent of gender-variant children will become transgendered adults. Mostly boys were studied and the majority were later defined as gay. These studies have been questioned because the subjects were gleaned from clinics overflowing with other psychological comorbidities. Nevertheless, the question is how to help the 8-to-10-year-old child who has been digging in their heels for five years or longer about their gender identity and gender role and is terrified about the prospect of puberty.

Despite the reality that "gender identity disorder" remains a DSM-IV psychiatric diagnosis, and though most major metropolitan areas have numerous mental health specialists skilled in the evaluation and counseling of late teens, young adults, and adults, precious few are competent to deal with preadolescents or their parents. Despite the tendency of pediatricians to refer complex issues such as gender variance in young children to child psychiatrists who have the most lengthy training, few have had any experience with primary gender identity disorders. Many are inclined to focus on and treat the presenting symptoms of depression and anxiety rather than the underlying gender conflict, and they frequently label the child's mood disorder as "bipolar."

If there are few competent mental health professionals for the young gender-variant child, there are even fewer pediatricians, adolescent specialists, or pediatric endocrinologists familiar with the pharmacologic methods of pubertal suppression and the administration of "cross-hormones," the sex steroids of the affirmed gender. Only recently has the subject of gender identity issues not linked to Disorders of Sex Development (formerly known as intersex) become a topic for discussion in pediatric and endocrinology academic meetings in North America. In western Europe, it is already on their agenda.

Pediatric endocrinologists are the specialists most familiar with the medications and hormones that retard or accelerate puberty, and these specialists play a pivotal role in the painful decisions about medical and surgical intervention consequent to the evaluation of the child whose genitals are ambiguous or variable. In some cases, a gender may be "assigned" that is at variance with the genotypic or gonadal sex. Several notorious cases in the past two decades reached the general public and had long-lasting influence on physicians' attitudes, because several young adults affirmed their genotypic gender identity and reversed their assignment. Criticism by adult former patients, some of whom formed their own support network, of their earlier treatment made pediatric endocrinologists and urologists defensive, and many questioned their ability to make decisions about these infants. Unable to hide from consultations on genital ambiguity, endocrinologists were even more reluctant to wade into the murkier waters of gender identity disorder, particularly when it was regarded as a psychiatric condition. Most hoped that the patients would remain in psychiatric care until they grew old enough to be treated by internal medicine–endocrinologists, who treat transgendered patients hormonally.

The power of the Internet and of international conferences and communiqués has enabled parents, mental health workers, and physicians to become aware of the skill with which the Dutch have delayed puberty and cross-hormone-treated over 100 adolescents. Suicide attempts, so frequent elsewhere, are almost unknown because parents and children know that they will be taken care of and will ultimately join a society known for its tolerance.

Yet, we remain at a crossroads, salivating at the prospect of applying the Dutch protocol for pubertal suppression, yet without permission from health insurers to pay for the expensive drugs or pressure from the medical and mental health communities to demand it. The frustration level of parents is rising, fueled by knowledge of what could be done. As with other relatively rare diseases and conditions, parents are usually ahead of the health professionals in knowledge and advocacy. To date there has been no manual of care written specifically for the parents of the transgendered child by people who have personal and professional experience. Now we finally have such a book, and it deserves a place in the office or home of everyone who is involved with transgendered children and their parents: health professionals, community workers, teachers and school administrators, and, of course, parents and relatives.

Norman P. Spack MD
Senior Associate, Endocrine Division
Children's Hospital Boston
Dept. of Pediatrics, Harvard Medical School

Introduction

"MOM, I'VE ALREADY TOLD YOU, I'm a girl, so stop saying HE!"

Alejandro had tried to tell his parents, from the time that he could barely talk, that he was really a girl. He would toddle into his older sister's closet to put on her dresses. He would wrap his hair in scarves and towels. He was always in his mom's makeup and shoes. At three, he regularly cried himself to sleep asking God why he made a mistake. By four, he spoke openly of wanting to kill himself, of not belonging in this world, of wanting to disappear. His parents initially thought it was just a phase, something every child goes through at some point. But when it didn't end, the only explanation they could think of was that he was probably gay. A counselor has since suggested that Alejandro may be transgender.

It took Nina's parents a number of years to realize that Nina always answered the question "Are you a boy or a girl?" the same way. She would say, "I am Nina." Initially, people thought her response was cute, but as she got older they started to feel that she was playing games with them by not answering the question. Furthermore, her parents started to get mad at her for being rude. Nina tried to explain that she didn't feel like a girl or a boy. Why did it matter—why couldn't she just be herself? Her parents firmly told her she was a girl, thinking it might settle the matter. Unfortunately, it was not so easy for Nina. Every time she had to choose a gender, as when lining up by boys and girls in class, she felt anguished and it was hard for her to follow instructions. Eventually, an insightful teacher made the connection when Nina started to wet her pants and stay in the coatroom right before lineup time. A child psychiatrist has brought up the idea that Nina may feel nongendered, or multigendered, or be gender-fluid.

Do these stories ring a bell? Throughout history, there have been children who challenged traditional gender definitions. But parenting practices and societal expectations have often caused those children to hide their identities from others and sometimes even from themselves.

The terrain of gender is expanding as times change. Today, it is much more difficult to justify telling your child who she is or isn't when the damage caused by denying her personal truth is so painfully obvious. More than ever before, people are coming to understand that the narrow confines we have given to gender are in many ways arbitrary. Science is researching what exactly is innate and what is culturally formed, supported, and enforced. Parents are faced now with the exciting and daunting task of raising children in a world that is expanding its understanding of gender.

Today, gender can no longer really be considered a two-option category. That form of thinking is outdated. It can be compared to trying to view the world in distinct racial categories without an understanding that an ever-growing percentage of the population is beautifully multiethnic. Gender is very similar. Most of us were taught, and most still firmly adhere to, the concept that there are only two distinct categories of gender, male and female. But in truth, many, if not most, of us are actually a blend.

Yet, allowing children to follow what is natural for them can be awkward and frightening for a parent when it means diverging from a trusted and familiar path. We as researchers, authors, and parents are aware of the difficulties parents face when first trying to understand and support a transgender or gender-variant child, and we know that in the end all parents want what is best for their children. We hope this book will provide caring families with helpful tools they can use to raise their gender-nonconforming children so they may feel more comfortable both in their bodies and in the world.

Are your eyes open? Are you ready to learn? Then you will see that children and teenagers can't help but show us that gender is really a spectrum. If we were to watch how children naturally unfold without the adult reinforcement—both conscious and subconscious—of gender roles and expectations, we would be in for a surprise. Many of the traits that we attribute to maleness or femaleness are taught and learned. Indeed, many aspects of gender are not innate at all but socially constructed. As many gender activists would say, you can buy your gender at the nearest clothing store.

So how do loving parents raise, support, and foster "gender-healthy" children? This is a complicated and often confusing task. In *The Transgender Child* we hope to begin this task by deepening your understanding of what exactly gender is. We will show you what we can all do to foster a healthy gender sense of self in children—within their own hearts and minds, within their families, within their schools, and within their communities. We can't understand terms such as *transgender* and *gender variance* if we don't understand what gender is.

Two big, necessary steps must be taken to effectively support, nurture and raise gender-variant and transgender children. The first is to thoroughly explore what is currently known and understood about gender. Once we become educated about the current thinking around gender itself, the next step is to release ourselves from our inherited beliefs, and thus allow ourselves to see the beautiful spectrum that gender really is. This learning and unlearning is important for all parents, not just parents with gender-variant children.

We want all families struggling with gender challenges to understand that they are not alone. Having felt for a while that it is high time a book be written for and available to parents of gender-variant and transgender children, we decided to write one together. We know there are thousands of other families facing the same challenges every day that many of you face. For all of you drowning in confusion, this book can serve as a life raft, teaching you methods to stay afloat. And for those of you who are already more confident in your parenting, this book will serve as validation that you are on the right track, and, we hope, provide you with new ideas and a fresh perspective.

We begin *The Transgender Child* by helping you discover if your child is likely transgender or gender-variant, defining our terms so that you can better understand the language used to discuss gender-variant children. We then go on to explore how to raise such a child, and how your family can best interact with the world. The book includes the most detailed and up-to-date information ever compiled in one resource for parents of transgender children and teens for dealing with the public school system and the medical system, including information on therapy and hormones. A chapter on legal issues, which has been checked for accuracy by the National Center for Lesbian Rights, is also included.

To provide you with the most reliable information, we have synthesized our knowledge in three different ways. First, *The Transgender Child* is inspired by both our years of personal experience with, and writing about, a wide variety of families raising gender-variant and transgender children and teens. Both of us have written extensively on topics including college issues for transgender teens, gender identity development in young children, and more general pregnancy and parenting subjects.

Second, the book is based on years of professional research that we have both done on topics such as social gender construction and how parenting and religious practices affect the health and well-being of gender-variant children and adults. Some of that research is explored here in the form of overviews and interviews, featuring quotes by experts in this field such as the activists Jenn Burtleton and Lydia Sausa, therapists Reid Vanderburgh and Jana L. Ekdahl, lawyers Shannon Price Minter and Jody Marksamer of the NCLR, Dr. Caitlin Ryan of the Family Acceptance Project, and endocrinologists Dr. Norman Spack, Dr. Nick Gorton, and Dr. Irene Sills. We thank these cutting-edge experts for their participation in—and belief in—this project. Organizations and institutions such as the Family Acceptance Project and The Park Day School have also influenced and inspired us.

Third, this book has been enriched by Stephanie's countless presentations to social workers, therapists, pediatricians, pediatric health care providers, public health providers, preschools, elementary schools, middle schools, high schools, college classes, and medical schools. Stephanie has conducted this work on her own and in conjunction with Gender Spectrum Education and Training. In short, this is a resource you can trust.

Finally, this book is also written for educators and professionals working with children. The information in this book can help deepen your understanding of gender-variant and transgender children, while teaching healthy practices that will create a safer environment for and meet the needs of all children and families. It can help you direct your professional practices as well as provide a valuable resource to the parents of the children in question.

As we leave you to explore the book, remember: All children are amazing, wonderful people who deserve unconditional love and support. We hope you agree.

Stephanie Brill
Rachel Pepper

Chapter 1

Is My Child Transgender?

*IT IS SO FUNNY when people ask me how I know I am a boy.
I just ask them, how do you know you're a boy? It's such a silly
question. You just know those things. I have known all my life!*
—Tommy, 7-year-old transgender boy

*As Andi's parents, we have been faced with two choices: we could
either choose to allow her to express herself and work to place her
in as supportive an environment as possible, or we could teach her
to suppress her true self, possibly leading to depression and low
self-worth. In other words, either she could fit the world, or we
could construct her world to fit her. We have made the choice to
fully support Andi to express exactly who she is, wherever that
path may lead.* —Parent of a 6-year-old transgender girl

There is a reason you have picked up this book. Most likely, you are
a parent raising a gender-variant or transgender child, or know someone who is. If so, you have questions about how to raise your child,
how to advocate for and support your child, and what the future will
hold for your child and your family. Or perhaps you are a teacher or
doctor or therapist working with a child who is gender-variant, or

even already affirmed as transgender. You may need further information on how to best understand and work with this child. Maybe you're really not sure what these gender terms mean, and what the differences may be between them, and you are ready to learn. In any case, you have probably recently asked yourself if your own child, or someone else's, was transgender, and you are ready for some answers.

How Common Are Transgender Kids?

No one knows how common transgender children are. Some gender specialists say that one in 500 children is significantly gender-variant or transgender. This may be a reasonable statistic, though the rate may actually be higher. Older studies, based only on statistics of postoperative transsexual men, say that the number is closer to 1 in 20,000. This figure is disputed by adult transgender activists today and seems to bear little relevance to the transgender and gender-variant children currently coming forth. Dr. Harvey Makadon of Harvard Medical School says gathering such statistics is almost impossible, as doctors cannot do "population-based research" in the US on such issues. So, at present, no one really knows how many transgender children there are.

How Can You Know a Child Is Transgender?

We know you may be hoping for a quick answer to the question "Is my child transgender?" But, as with many other issues in life, the answer can be complicated or may reveal itself to you only over time.

Luckily, most children are very clear on this subject. When given two choices—boy or girl—most kids feel strongly that they are one or the other. There are always children who do not feel like either or who feel like both, and if you provide more options for them, you will get a much wider range of responses. When your 18-month-old girl's first words are "me boy," or your 2-year-old son insists that he is a girl, and these responses don't waver or change over the next few years, you can be pretty sure that you have a transgender child. We are not saying that just because your toddler has said something cute or confusing you should immediately assume they are transgender. But if a toddler goes through a phase of insisting they are the opposite gender of their birth sex, and if this "phase" doesn't end, it is not a phase.

Dr. Norman Spack, an expert in this field and founder of the GeMS clinic at Children's Hospital Boston for children with disorders of sexual differentiation or who are transgender, notes that there are several important and clear ways young children typically reveal their transgender identity. He says to watch for bathroom behavior (does your little girl insist on peeing while standing up?), swimsuit aversion (most trans kids absolutely will not wear the bathing suit of their anatomical sex), what type and style of underpants kids select (does your son want the girl-cut panties with flowers on them?), and a strong desire to play with toys typically assigned to the opposite sex.

Spack considers these four points carefully when meeting a young child who may become a patient for the first time, and he has found these to be reliable markers for a transgender identity in children who cannot yet fully express in words what they are feeling. When all four behaviors are present, Spack says, "Everything just seems to line up. These kids are making a statement with their every move and word."

However, the vast majority of gender-variant children are not transgender; they are just gender-nonconforming. The parents, in an attempt to do right by their child, learn about transgender children and think their child must be transgender. This is not always the case. In fact, it is usually not the case. We will discuss gender-variant children, as well as transgender children, throughout the book.

Did I Cause This? Can I Stop It?

Parenting does not cause a person to be transgender or gender-variant. Transgender identity is not the result of divorce, child abuse, disappointment at the sex of the child, or being an overbearing parent, a lenient parent, or an absentee parent. Nothing a parent or guardian does, or does not do, can cause any child to become gender-variant or transgender. The studies that once implicated parenting in whether a person becomes transgender have all been widely disputed. They were based on thinking that is no longer commonly accepted in either the mental health care system or the medical establishment, as well as often lacking a clear distinction between gender-variant expression and transgender identity. If you encounter this form of thinking from your professionals, it is time to find new professionals with a more current, evidence-based practice. If a professional tells you that you can change your child to have a different gender identity, they are wrong. There is nothing anyone can do to change a child's gender identity. It is a core part of self. However, your parenting of your child can influence how your child feels about themselves in relation to their gender identity.

At this point, before we dig deeper, we would like to define some terms you will be seeing throughout the book:

biological or anatomical sex: Biological sex refers to a person's physical anatomy and is used to assign gender at birth. Although most people believe there are only two options—male and female—this is not true. There is a range of possible variations in human anatomy and chromosomal makeup.

gender identity: Gender identity refers to a person's internalized, deeply felt sense of being male, female, both, or neither. It can be different from the biological sex assigned at birth. Because gender identity is internal and personally defined, it is not visible to others—it is determined by the individual alone. Most people have an early sense of their gender identity, and if it is not congruous with their anatomical sex they may begin voicing this between the ages of 2 and 4.

gender expression: In contrast to gender identity, which is an internal feeling, gender expression is how we externalize our gender. It encompasses everything that communicates our gender to others: clothing, hairstyles, mannerisms, how we speak, how we play, and our social interactions and roles.

gender variance/gender nonconformity: Gender variance refers to behaviors and interests that fall outside what is considered normal for a person's assigned biological sex. This may be indicated by choices in games, clothing, and playmates, or it may take the form of the child stating and restating that they wish to be the other sex—for example, a girl who insists on having short hair and prefers to play football with the boys, or a boy who wears dresses and wishes to wear his hair long. It should be noted that gender variance does not typically apply to children who have only a brief, passing curiosity in trying out these behaviors or interests.

transgender/cross-gender: These terms, which are used interchangeably, refer to an individual whose gender identity does not match their assigned birth gender. For example, a transgender child self-identifies as a girl but is biologically male. Being cross-gender or transgender does not imply any specific sexual orientation. Therefore, transgender and cross-gender people may additionally identify as straight, gay, lesbian, or bisexual.

sexual orientation: Sexual orientation refers to the gender of the persons one is attracted to romantically or sexually. Sexual orientation and gender identity are separate, distinct parts of a person's identity. Although your child may not yet be aware of their sexual orientation, they usually have a strong sense of their gender identity.

affirmed male/transboy: A child or adult who was born anatomically female but has a male gender identity; a term used by some medical professionals for a transgender boy or man.

affirmed female/transgirl: A child or adult who was born anatomically male but has a female gender identity; a term used by some medical professionals for a transgender girl or woman.

gender fluidity: Gender fluidity conveys a wider, more flexible range of gender expression, with personal appearance and behaviors that may even change from day to day. For some children, gender fluidity extends beyond behavior and interests, and actually serves to specifically define their gender identity. In other words, a child may feel they are a girl some days and a boy on others, or possibly feel that neither term describes them accurately.

genderqueer: The term *genderqueer* represents a blurring of the lines around both gender identity and sexual orientation. Genderqueer people embrace a fluidity of gender expression and sexual orientation. This term is really an adult identifier; it is not typically used in connection with gender identity in preadolescent children.

What Is Gender?

A fundamental understanding of gender is important to raising gender-nonconforming children and teens in a supportive manner.

Attitudes toward gender and what is seen as gender-appropriate behavior are formed in early childhood. These formative views may change, but they influence choices and decisions made throughout life. In other words, how you learned and interacted with gender as a young child directly influences how you view the world today. Some of what we have to share about gender may initially seem radical because of the lens through which you currently perceive gender. You may come away from this book wondering what the essence of being male or female really is, and asking yourself why no one has ever really discussed gender with you before.

Gender is all around us, and it is actually taught to us, from the moment we are born. Talking with and reading about gender-variant children and teens, as well as raising them and interacting with them, changes your personal experience of gender. As your understanding of gender variance deepens, so will your ability to discuss the subject with greater ease. Your greater ease and comfort with the subject and with your child will put others at ease. This is enormously helpful in lessening the fears, confusion, and judgment of others.

There is a learning curve for everyone who interacts with gender-variant and transgender people. This is understandable. Significant gender variance confuses the foundation of the gendered social order. Therefore, it confuses the internal sense of what feels natural. Our purpose is to help you navigate this new terrain—to move smoothly through the stages of parental acceptance, which may include denial and grief, to the goal of integration and celebration.

So, what *is* gender? Let's start with a very brief exercise. Grab a pencil and paper and write down your answers to the following questions:

- What is a boy?
- What is a girl?
- How do you know?
- When does a person know that they are a boy or a girl?
- Are you a male? Are you a female? How do you know?
- Are you, or parts of you, both? How do you know?
- If your anatomy changed overnight to the opposite sex, would it change who you feel yourself to be?

Put your responses aside for now, but keep them in mind as you continue to read this chapter. It is helpful to do this exercise periodically, as your answers to these questions may change over time.

Gender is not actually inherently connected to one's bodily anatomy. Biological sex and gender are different. This is a very important distinction—most people have been told from as young as they can remember that sex and gender are the same thing. In fact, gender is a societal construct. Our society acknowledges only two gender categories: male or female. This binary view of gender is burdened with expectations and rules for each category. These rules dictate the standards for clothing, activities, and behaviors, though as the previous exercise may have revealed to you, one's clothing style, choice of activities,

Gender Diversity Worldwide

There is irrefutable evidence that transgender people have existed in most, if not all, cultures worldwide. Although this history is still being rediscovered, a solid body of scholarly work already exists.

Writers such as Will Roscoe have extensively documented Native American people in North America and their inclusion of and even occasional reverence for gender-variant people. Such people were sometimes considered to have special spiritual powers, and male children who displayed feminine qualities at a young age were often apprenticed to a shaman to become healers. *Two-spirit,* a specific term for third-gender folks, is used by many lesbian, gay, bisexual, transgender, or intersex Native Americans. It can also describe those who exhibit a balance of masculine and feminine energies, and it is not always used exclusively for transgender people.

Leslie Feinberg, a well-known transgender activist and writer, is the author of *Transgender Warriors.* The book gives an overview of transgender people in native cultures worldwide, with amazing accompanying photographs and archival illustrations.

Scientists such as Joan Roughgarden, a Stanford biologist, transwoman, and author of *Evolution's Rainbow: Diversity, Gender and Sexuality in Nature and People,* are also shedding light on the variety of expressions found in animal and human nature. Roughgarden's book includes several sections on transgendered people, like the Polynesian *mahu* ("half-man half-woman") and Indian *hijras* (male-to-female transgendered persons who constitute an entire religious sect and caste), among others. She also describes rituals performed in tribes such as the Navajo and Papago that served to bless young two-spirit persons and also to

> test their resolve to remain their birth gender or assume a different one.
>
> Unfortunately, what these books also make clear is how native cultures with accepting attitudes toward gender variance have been attacked and overtaken, driven by the religious and political motivation of others. In the process, all over the world, transgender people have had to hide themselves to survive. Yet, the evidence is insurmountable that human gender identity and behavior have always existed across a wide spectrum.

or modes of behavior may not fit exclusively into the male or the female category.

What we expect of a male or a female person is created for the most part by the culture. Gender roles have provided a structure for our society by establishing commonly understood ways of functioning and interacting with one another.

The feminist movement has addressed the inequity of these expected social gender roles. By examining cultural stereotypes, the feminist movement has opened many doors for both women and men. Today there is a more egalitarian division of domestic duties, sex-based discrimination is against the law, and sexual harassment is no longer a commonly accepted form of social interaction. But we haven't gone quite far enough yet— women have not reached full equality in the work world, women and men are still restricted to the clothes that are culturally available to them, and men are often not accepted as nurturing, full-time caretakers of children.

Social Gender Role Development: Gender Role Acquisition and Pressures to Conform

Children are heavily influenced by the gender lessons their parents and society teach them. Parents, both actively and passively, consciously and

What about Intersex People?

The term *intersex* refers to persons born with less than clearly defined, or some combination of, external genitalia or internal sexual organs. Many different medical terms are given to intersex conditions (now often called disorders of sex development, or DSD), including congenital adrenal hyperplasia, classic hermaphroditism, and hypospadia. Some intersex people are believed to have differing chromosomal combinations from the classic female (XX) and male (XY). Intersex babies are sometimes arbitrarily assigned a sex and a gender at birth, based often on a single medical opinion, and surgeries have been performed to more clearly align a baby's genitalia to match a typical female or male child's anatomy.

The greatest similarities between intersex and transgender people is that both groups of people may experience discomfort in their own body, feel as though they were "assigned" the wrong sex, and often seek surgery or hormones to correct this. Because others decide the gender of a baby born intersex, these children may grow up feeling a disconnect between what they are told about their body and how they feel inside. Or, they may feel there is something inherently wrong with their genitalia, notice that their genitals are not like other people's, or have problems with sexual or reproductive functions as they mature.

Transgender people share similar feelings of discomfort in their bodies, such as being born into the "wrong" body, and wish for a way to fix this, although their genitalia and reproductive anatomy are usually typical of their birth sex. Additionally, in Western culture, both conditions have historically been considered shameful pathologies best endured in secret, corrected by doctors or psychologists bent on "fixing" the "problem."

Yet groups such as the Intersex Society of North America (ISNA) advise against too strong a comparison between transgender people and those born intersex. They believe most intersex people do not have conflict about their gender and suffer different discriminations from transgender people. ISNA currently recommends assigning intersex babies a birth gender but not performing any surgeries until children can decide for themselves which sex they wish to identify more strongly with. Biologist Joan Roughgarden and others take the position that both intersexuality and transgenderism should be seen as normal human conditions. Transgender and intersex people share a new history of speaking out, organizing, and determining their own biological destinies, and they are finally beginning to be seen as merely two variations on an amazingly diverse spectrum of gender and anatomy.

For further information: The Intersex Society of North America, www.isna.org.

subconsciously, are involved in teaching boys how to be boys and girls how to be girls.

Children mimic what they see around them. Through our interactions with them, children learn gender-appropriate behavior, they absorb contextual roles of power and acceptable patterns of desire. They selectively attend to and imitate models of the same sex. How a child perceives gender may change over time and is directly influenced by class, ethnicity, age, religion, and culture. Even young children are attuned to their culture's idealized versions of male and female.

Gendered interactions begin as soon as parents know the sex of their baby. Studies have shown that even before birth, and certainly afterward, adults speak differently in tone and content to a newborn based on the perceived gender of the baby. With anatomically female babies or babies of unknown sex, adults use a more singsong tone, and these babies are held and comforted more. Baby boys are spoken to in lower tones, and often held and comforted less. Most adults are completely unaware of these differences in their interactions with babies.

Gender is socially constructed and monitored. Practically everything is assigned a gender, even colors, toys, clothes, and behaviors. Through a combination of social conditioning and personal preference, by age 3 most children prefer activities and behaviors typically associated with their sex.

Accepted social gender roles and expectations of gender expression are so entrenched in our culture that most people cannot imagine a civilized society without them. Because gender is such an inherent part of the societal fabric, most gender-typical people have never questioned exactly what gender is. They have never had to, because the system has worked for them.

When a person's preferences and self-expression fall outside commonly understood gender norms, we call this *gender variance*. Gender variance is a normal part of human expression, documented across cultures and recorded history. When a child emerges as gender-variant, the problem lies not with the child nor with its parenting, but with a social system that places rigid limits on gender expression.

The currently accepted binary system of gender adversely affects gender-nonconforming children. The first step in understanding and supporting gender-nonconforming children is to grasp the concept that gender and anatomy are not the same, and furthermore, that gender is a blend of both social norms and inherent core identity.

Core Identity Development

Psychologists believe that a person's core identity has three major components. It is believed these distinct parts of the self are set in place during childhood by age 6, and then revisited as a teenager.

The three components are:

Gender identity—your deep inner feeling of gender, regardless of anatomy

Style of behavior—your natural inclinations and expressions

Sexual orientation—whom you are attracted to

It is essential to understand that these parts of core identity are separate and distinct from one another. In the majority of people, all three components of identity are aligned. This dominant configuration is the social context from which gender roles and the system of gender are constructed, and in Western culture it has come to be the standard expectation. But in truth, a great many people vary in one or more of these aspects of core identity. We all know well-adjusted adults who have a mixture of identities.

For example:

- You probably know a male (gender identity) who is gentle and emotional (style of behavior) and who is heterosexual (sexual orientation)
- You may know a woman (gender identity) who has a crew cut and works construction (style of behavior) and who is a lesbian (sexual orientation)
- You may know a person you perceive to be female, but who actually perceives herself as androgynous (gender identity), who has long hair, wears miniskirts, is a high-powered executive (style of behavior) and who is bisexual (sexual orientation)

Of course, each child forms their social identity in a wide context that includes ethnicity, class, culture, and religion. These additional factors in identity can have strong influences on social gender development and especially on a child's inner sense of being "bad" or "wrong" if parts of their core identity do not align with their community's ethnic, racial, or religious expectations.

Gender Identity

One component of a person's core identity is their gender identity. Gender identity refers to your personal sense of self and where you fit on the continuum of male to female. It is intimately related to social gender roles—the expectations placed by society on behaviors and appearances—but gender identity is the self-label. It is who you know yourself to be.

It is most commonly understood that gender identity is formed in the brain. Some theories point to environmental influences, others to prenatal hormonal influence, but most agree that it is most likely determined before we are born. From this perspective, the brain is a gendered organ, and gender identity is not a conscious decision. People do not choose to feel like a boy or a girl, or like both, or neither. They simply are who they are. From this perspective, transgender people and all people whose gender identity does not align with their anatomical sex are simply born this way.

What Makes a Person Transgender?

I want the world to see that this is truly who my child is. All the books and theories and research in the world pale compared to this simple reality: see my child as herself, and you will know you have seen the real child. This is no act, no dysfunction, no illness. This is a child in all her glory finding her true path in this world.
—Parent of a 6-year-old transgirl

There's something different about their wiring. But we really don't know what makes a person transgender, any more than we know what makes people lesbian or gay. —Dr. Norman Spack, Children's Hospital Boston

No one yet knows what makes some people transgender. Transgender people have been documented throughout history, throughout cultures.

Some live open lives, others keep their transgender identity to themselves and do not feel safe externally expressing their true self, and still others hide their identities completely and are not discovered until after death. Being transgender is a normal variance of human expression. It may not serve you to try to search for a cause, as this seems to indicate that there is a "problem." When you are struggling to accept your child, it is important to realize that there have always been gender-variant and transgender people.

Transgender people are of all ethnicities, races, and religions. They are raised by all kinds of parents, in all different kinds of environments. Current thinking on this topic does lean toward the idea that one cause of transgender identity involves exposure to prenatal maternal hormones. Of course, this idea can be disputed in cases of twins where only one twin is transgender. Other theories suggest that a high percentage of transgender children are conceived using in vitro fertilization, or that there is a chromosomal anomaly among transgender people, or that transgender people may have biological parents who are bipolar. Some people argue that being transgender is genetic, and while it's true that some families contain an unusually high number of transgender people, most transgender people do not have any other trans family members (that they know of).

Since openly expressed transgender identity is on the rise, some wonder if environmental factors are increasing the incidence of transgenderism. Or does increased access to hormone therapy and surgery make transgender people more likely to self-disclose? Is it due to increased parental and societal awareness? Each of these explanations seems as logical as the next, and there is likely truth in them all. In other words, we don't actually know what makes a person transgender. But it is understood to be biological and not "caused" socially.

Typical Ages at Which a Child Realizes They Are Transgender

Childhood

> He was a little baby of about 18 months and his first formed sen-
> tence was "Me a boy mama." I gave him a bottle because I
> assumed he said "Me baba mama," but he threw the baba down
> and repeated himself. I thought it was cute, how he was always
> confused, but I knew something was up. He was always wanting
> 'boyish' type toys, and I had a feeling he was different from my
> older three daughters. —Parent of a 7-year-old transboy

> He may refer to himself as a boy but say he wishes he were a girl.
> He has asked how old he can be before he can have his "pee-pee"
> cut off. —Aunt of a gender-variant 6-year-old boy

Because gender identity emerges around the same time as a child learns
to speak, it is common for children who are transgender to try to let
their parents know this when they are very, very young. It may take a
number of years for parents to understand the depth of what their child
is really expressing. At first parents think it's cute. Then they often think
their child is confused: "No, honey, boys have a penis and girls have a
vagina." They may do this even while a child displays severe trauma
about their anatomy. And all parents reasonably assume that the "confusion" must be a phase. Over time, parents of transgender children
come to recognize that this "phase" is not changing.

A young child's ability to outwardly express their gender identity
is predominantly controlled by their parents. Again, parents cannot
control the actual inner experience of their child. If the child has a
cross-gender identity, it won't change just because the parents don't
accept it. However, with clear communications of parental rejection,
over time the child's cross-gender identity may go underground and
become internalized with shame. So for a transgender child to be able
to experience a positive sense of self requires the support of the par-

ents. As it is developmentally appropriate for all toddlers and young children to assert their gender identity, a transgender toddler or young child will likewise naturally continue to assert their gender identity. For example, a cross-gender young child may verbally assert their gender, correcting people who refer to them with the inappropriate pronoun. When they reach preschool, they may go to the dress-up corner to find clothes that better reflect their inner gender. They may try to change their name. Their play may revolve around expression of the gender they feel themselves to be. They may throw temper tantrums if they cannot have the clothes or toys or other accoutrements associated with their gender identity.

> *At first, we thought Andi's desire to wear dresses was just a phase . . . After some time, we realized this was not a phase, but part of her identity. When she was almost 4, she slowly started wanting to hide the fact that she was born a boy. For instance, she would get angry at us if someone assumed she was a girl and we corrected them. In preschool, she started wearing oversize T-shirts, pretending they were dresses. She then moved on to a "ballerina skirt" which she made by layering her mom's undershirt underneath a kid's shirt. Soon enough, she became distraught that the outfit "wasn't right." One day, she just cried and cried about it. She was inconsolable. We finally bought her a dress her size.*
> —Parent of a 6-year-old transgirl

Of course, at such a young age, it can be a challenge for parents to determine whether their child is gender-variant or actually transgender. But because the social regulations for the preferences of boys are so strict, if your boy child prefers feminine self-expression and play and is not insisting that he is a girl, it is most likely that he is just gender-variant. Boys are much more socially restricted than girls in terms of personal expression in most levels of society. Thus, just because your boy prefers dresses, it does not mean that he is transgender, or gay. At this point it simply means he likes dresses. Do not be too quick to label your child as transgender. Take the time to truly observe what is coming from your child. This may take several years. Do not push for an answer. We will discuss this throughout the book.

Preteen and Early Adolescence

The next typical time for transgender identity to emerge is just before and during early puberty, so depending on the child, between 9 and 14 years old. At this age, children begin to experience hormonal and physical changes toward maturation, and huge alerts go off in their brains. When this happens, kids this age usually try to announce their disquietude to their parents in one way or another. Likewise, parents may notice something amiss with their child and take them to a therapist for withdrawal, acting out, depression, or self-mutilation. During the therapeutic process the gender identity issue comes forth. Most of these parents look back and say they had suspected that their child was going to be gay or lesbian, but they never considered that their child might be transgender.

> *My 9-year-old daughter just announced one day that she is really a boy and her new name was Jack. She had this attitude that I would just accept this. I couldn't believe it. At first I thought it was a joke, and I ignored it. But that weekend she wanted to shop for boys' clothes. I humored her, as our family had recently been through a messy divorce and I thought this was her way of getting attention. What harm would it do to get her boys' clothes? Then she started to cry every time I called her Joanne. I got a call from her teacher saying Joanne was now going by Jack at school and was telling everyone she is transgender and really a boy. The teacher wanted to know what I wanted her to do. I didn't know what to say. I went to a parent support group. They were all so accepting and asked me if I was*

mourning my daughter. I just thought, Hell no, I haven't lost her. I thought they were a bunch of wackos.

It's been a year now, and Jack is Jack. I have a lot of sadness and confusion, still. But I love Jack and he is happy. I am not ready to talk about medicines and surgeries; I just can't go there now. But our doctor, and the parents in my support group (yes, I went back) tell me I should think about it. There are options that could make Jack's life easier for him and aren't permanent.

I do realize that Jack feels he is a boy. Sometimes I call my mom and just cry. Everyone tells me I am not to blame, but I am not so sure. There must be some reason my daughter feels he is a boy. You see—I am so screwed up with my pronouns. I always thought Joanne would be a lesbian—she actually doesn't look or act that different as Jack. But it is true, she seems happier. Some days I feel like this is all my problem. I hope to wake up and have it all be different. Other days I wonder, So what's the big deal? He finds it suits him to be a boy. I know I'll be learning about those medicines soon. His breasts are beginning to grow ever so slightly and I realize that if I don't support him fully, I may lose him alto-gether. —Parent of a 10-year-old transboy

My son had been so depressed. He had experienced some relief from his depression when he told us he was gay. He seemed to be happy for the first time in a year. He left his computer and actually did an after-school activity. But then the depression hit again. We worried he was getting harassed at school. He reported that it was no worse than ever. He has always been harassed because he wears rather flamboyant clothes, and speaks very expressively with his body and hands. He said he wanted to die because he couldn't imagine life continuing in the way he was living it. He had no will to live.

We sent him to a therapist. Months into therapy, there was a day I will never forget for the rest of my life. He went into therapy

that day as Russell, he came out as Heather. It was a long ther-
apy session that extended into three hours—with me invited in
for the last hour or so. During that time his therapist helped Rus-
sell to realize that he actually felt and truly believed he was a girl.

When his therapist said that some people are transgender,
and that it is nothing to be afraid of, Russell came forth with his
alter ego, Heather. He said that Heather has lived inside of him
for years. And she needs to be out. I can't tell you it's been easy.
That would be a blatant lie. My family was falling apart. My
husband and our other children did not accept that Russell was
transgender. Our home felt like a war zone. The final straw hap-
pened when Heather got beaten up at school. It was pretty bad.
She was injured and shaken. When her father got home he said,
"Well, what did you expect?" The silence was deadly. Finally, in
a quiet voice, Heather said she was leaving. If she wasn't loved
here, she would leave in the morning. I announced to my hus-
band in bed that night that I would be leaving, too. I would not
send our child out into the world believing she was not loved.

That did it. It is embarrassing to say that it got so out of hand,
but it did. And honestly, I don't think we are the only ones. I have
talked to other parents who have also gotten too close to losing
their kids. We all love Heather. Heather took the rest of that year
off and did volunteer work as she started her estrogen. She is
starting tenth grade at a new school, as a girl. —Parent of a
15-year-old transgirl

Late Adolescence

The third typical time for transgender self-realization during childhood is
the end of adolescence, when the other parts of the self have emerged more
fully and gender identity becomes clear. Before that point, many teenagers
try on different sexualities to see what fits best, not realizing that the inner
mismatch is not about sexual orientation but rather about gender.

In the summer, right before starting at a new private high school her junior year, our daughter told us she was transgender. We didn't know how to respond. We acted on the fly. The first thing we said was that we would always love her no matter what. I am so glad that we were able to respond in such a mature way. We have always told our kids we would love them no matter what they did, so this was no different. We were really worried for her. We did not want her to have to go through the hassles—and worse—that she would have to go through in her high school if she "transitioned" to a boy. So after many more talks, we told her that we would support her through this. However, we insisted that she go to therapy and that she meet other transgender adults. If she still felt she was transgender, then we would pay for her breast removal surgery as a graduation present, she could take testosterone over the summer, and she could go to college as a boy.

We thought we were so liberal. We were proud of this response. Our close friends were in awe of our calm way of handling the situation. But this was not good enough for our daughter. When the first report card came we thought they had made a mistake. We actually called the school and told them they had sent us the wrong report card. This one was about Bradley—our daughter was Brandy. They were confused; they said Bradley had told them that they had misprinted his name on the application and that his name was actually Bradley—not Brandy. This was how we found out that our daughter had been living as a boy full-time out in the world. We went to her job—and there she was for all to see with a name tag that said "Bradley." It was obvious only to us that our daughter was binding her breasts and presenting herself as a boy to the world. To anyone looking she was obviously a teenage boy.

We felt so betrayed. We had been so generous in our acceptance of her transgender identity. Why had she gone behind our backs? When we confronted her, Bradley looked at us like we were from the moon. She said to us, "You have always told me to be exactly who I am. You have told me all my life to resist peer pressure and to stand up for what is true and right. When it came time for you to do the same, for you to stand up for me—you couldn't. That wasn't going to stop me from standing up for myself. Who did you think you raised? A coward?"

What could we say to that? —Parents of a 17-year-old transboy

Of course, there are some people who begin a gender transition as an adult. Usually they always knew something was different, even as a child, but hadn't known it was a transgender identity. They may have thought that they were lesbian or gay, but then realized that this wasn't quite right. Or, fearing or facing familial rejection, they tried as hard as they could to believe they were not transgender. As times change, we anticipate that most transgender people will develop the awareness and ability to transition before full adulthood.

Being Transgender Is Not a Choice

No one chooses to be transgender. It is not cool. It is not easy. It has no allure. Children and teens alike do not try it on for size like a pair of shoes. Being transgender is one of the most difficult things to be because it is not understood and the binary gender system is so pervasive.

When a child or teen asserts that they are transgender, you must listen. As a parent, stop to gather more information and truly listen to what your child is saying to you. If your child has told you this and you responded with denial, or by assuming it's a phase, it's not too late. Go back to your child with open arms and an open heart and ask for clarification. Keep the lines of communication open.

People are who they are. We cannot control that. But parents do have the power to love and accept and support their children uncondi-

Stephanie and others with Gender Spectrum hold workshops in school classrooms to discuss gender. They explain that anatomy and gender are different, that sometimes a person who has been told they are a boy may feel like a girl, or vice versa. Then they ask for a show of hands from the kids who feel that they are a boy, those who feel that they are a girl, and those who feel that they are some of both. The results are pretty amazing, especially in the younger grades. The younger the children, the more hands go up saying they are some of both. We cannot help but conclude that many children have a gender identity that is much more fluid than we leave room for.

tionally. It is a parent's job to love, nurture and nourish their wonderful children. It's just that all parents are sometimes misguided by fear and confuse that with love. In the next chapter we will review exactly what parents can do to best support their gender-nonconforming and cross-gender children.

Style of Behavior

Psychologists have identified one's style of behavior as another component of core identity. A person's style of behavior reflects their natural inclinations and expressions, and society labels these preferences by gender. Thus the core part of our identity that is reflected in our own unique style of behavior can also be seen as gender expression and presentation.

Markers of style of behavior include hairstyles, body language, ways of walking and moving through space, clothing preferences, and styles of play. The greater the inclination and preference for behavior considered to be of and for the other gender, the greater the variance. For example, a boy with long hair who prefers to wear bright-pink shirts and soft cotton flower-print pants is often perceived as a girl based on the gender cues of presentation. These personal preferences for expression mark this child as significantly gender-variant or gender-nonconforming.

Parents and children both are judged when a child expresses preferences that are seen as belonging to the other gender. In mainstream culture this is especially true when a child born biologically male expresses interests or behaviors traditionally considered feminine. However, in many ethnic and religious cultures girls are equally restricted in their accepted styles of behavior.

This social pressure affects not only the child, but also the child's parents. With boys, because the expressions of masculinity are so tightly monitored, fathers often have a more challenging time accepting gender variance in their sons. Furthermore, many people see children as reflections of their parents; thus a more feminized boy can be perceived as a threat to the father's own masculinity. In cultures where the expressions of femininity are tightly monitored, a girl with gender-variant tendencies is often considered a great shame to the family.

What Is Gender Fluidity?

Some kids simply are not typical boys or girls. They are also not transgender. They may like things that are thought of as boy's things one day, and things that are considered girl's things another. They may want to wear boy clothes one day and girl clothes the next. These kids may even say they feel like a boy one day, and like a girl the next.

Some children are simply more fluid by their nature. They do not feel comfortable fitting into the established boxes of behavior. They may move from one box to the next and back again or say that neither box feels right.

What Should I Do If My Child Is Gender-fluid?

If your child is gender-fluid, you have a challenging task at hand: to resist the urge to make them choose. The agony of not being able to label their children can cause some parents such stress that they actually would prefer their child to be transgender. Yes, it may seem easier to have a transgender child or a typically gendered child—but that is not what you have. Remember to resist the urge to make your child choose for your greater ease.

> *My child has always identified with girls and often likes to dress in girl's clothes at home, but is quite clear that he is a boy and does not want to be identified as a girl. I don't see him as transgender at this time, and I hold myself open to wherever he lands on the spectrums of gender identity and sexual orientation in the future. He told me long ago that he just wanted to "be myself," which has guided me since in my parenting of him.* —Parent of a gender-variant young boy

> *My son is gender-variant. He knows he is a boy and sometimes likes boy stuff, but then he also loves to dress up as a girl and do girl stuff—so far no clear-cut indication that he wants to be a boy or a girl, or which gender he might decide on.* —Parent of a 7-year-old gender-variant boy

Stay with the unsettled feelings and support your child. Be their advocate. And remember, even those of us who are typically gendered do not wear the same clothes every day, and do not like to do the same things every day. The same is true for children. Gender-fluid kids need support in fending off pressures from other people to remain in a more predictable gender state. They need your love and encouragement that they can be just who they are. Equip your kids with the skills to recognize and respond effectively to bullying. Advocate for them at school and out in the world. Be their supporters.

Over time your child may choose a gender or gender presentation that is more comfortable for you. They may conform in response to social pressure, or they may naturally find a resting place that works for them.

Or they may not, and they may remain gender-fluid throughout their lifetime. It is impossible to say how your child will feel in relation to their gender next week, next year, or 10 years from now. Regardless, they will thrive with the reassurance of your love and support.

Gender-variant Children Who Feel More Comfortable Living a Cross-gender Life

Most gender-variant children are not transgender. They have varying degrees of atypical expression and self-presentation—but it is primarily their social gender that is nonconforming rather than their internal sense of gender. Gender-variant children need a lot of support being in the world. The support they need increases with the degree of variance.

Sometimes support at home is not enough. The pressures of society can be very heavy on a gender-nonconforming child. It can be too much for any child to bear. Sometimes, with the additional support of a school that supports gender variance and includes it in their educational philosophy, and with an accepting extended family and friend network, even a significantly gender-variant child can withstand the outside world's pressures. Guided by their child, some families lessen the burden their child has to bear simply by not correcting erroneous perceptions and thus avoiding negativity.

However, a complex coping response can develop with gender-variant children if they do not receive enough support for being who they are. Some of these children find that it is easier to be transgender than to be the gender-variant person that they are. This seems especially true for biological males who have feminine preferences and traits. It is hard to imagine how a society could pressure a child to be transgender when being transgender is not socially accepted and understood in most of society. This is sometimes more easily understood through case stories. Stephanie's work with Marlow's family comes to mind.

Marlow has always preferred feminine forms of expression, but his parents found different degrees of comfort with his nature. For example, they would let him have long hair, but only to a certain length. They allowed him to play with Kim Possible™ dolls, but not Barbies™. They allowed him colorful clothing, but no dresses. When he was 4 they bought him his first baby doll. Their son was ecstatic. The parents realized it wasn't a big deal—why not? It's just a doll and kids should be able to play with whatever they want, right? So they allowed him more options. Soon he was wearing clothes from the girl's department. Still no dresses, but pants, fabrics, and patterns reserved in our culture for girls. Others were perceiving him as female. His parents allowed him to wear his hair however he wanted it. It grew long and he started to wear barrettes.

Throughout all this time, he never said he felt like a girl. In fact, he would correct anyone who referred to him as female. He felt strong in his male identity; he just liked the presentation and appearance typically thought of as female. Over time, he began to show distinct signs of anxiety when people would visibly recoil upon finding out he was a boy. He began to dread going out in public. He would cry to his family about why he couldn't look the way he wanted and be a boy, why everyone thought he was a girl or wanted him to be one. He was feeling social pressure to conform. While his internal sense was already firmly male, social gender rules were pressuring him to look like a boy. Over time, he became more comfortable not telling people he was a boy to avoid a negative reaction. Seemingly in response to this, he started to ask his parents not to correct strangers who perceived him as female. He didn't want to be a spectacle wherever he went; he just wanted to be himself.

Finally, in the middle of first grade, the pressure became too great and he decided to conform. He asked his parents to cut his hair, and it was cut much shorter, back to an acceptable long hairstyle for boys rather than down his back. He decided to dress in clothes purchased in the boys' department. He chose to keep his same toys, as that was personal and no one would have to know what he played with when he wasn't at school.

But what followed was a progressive depression. Six-year-old Marlow eventually became so withdrawn and sad that he would hardly communicate. At first his teachers were so relieved by the transformation in
him. Marlow was no longer the object of ridicule—they no longer had
to monitor the playground for older children teasing him. But over time,
Marlow stopped participating in class. The sparkle went out of his eyes—
in fact, he stopped making eye contact at all. He withdrew socially.
Whereas he used to play with both girls and boys at lunch and recess,
he took to sitting alone on a bench and reading a book. The teachers
realized they had a serious problem on their hands.

Marlow's parents put some of his old bright, colorful clothes back in
his drawers with the boy clothes. Marlow came screeching out of his
room saying, "Don't do this to me. It hurts, it hurts. People don't love me
when I dress in those clothes. But I don't love me when I dress in these
clothes. I can't do this anymore. I just want to die."

Not knowing what else to do, with a potentially suicidal child on their
hands, his parents and their family therapist started to do some research
together. They came to the realization that though Marlow was not typically transgender, he was also not typically gendered. They decided to
take a leap of faith and see if Marlow would prefer to live as a girl than as
a boy. After many talks together as a family and with the therapist, they
agreed that though Marlow didn't really feel he was a girl inside, he
wanted to be able to be himself, and he had always liked the same things.
Trying to dress and act like a boy to make other people more comfortable
was making him miserable. Enough people had told him he had to be a
girl to be the way he wanted, so he was ready. He was ready to be a girl.

When Marlow became Marla and transferred to the public school in
the next district, her whole world changed. The parents had their vibrant
child back. They had essentially exchanged their son for a daughter, but
nothing had really changed except the name and pronoun. Their child
was still the same, only no longer anxious, depressed, or suicidal—this
child was happy.

Marla is living a cross-gender life. She finds it much easier as a girl. And now, at 8, she can't imagine living life as a boy. She says, "I never felt like a boy, I always felt like a girl. Finally other people understand me for who I am."

In a situation like Marlow/Marla's we won't know until later in life if this child will always feel this way, or if it was a coping mechanism at the time. Or we may never know. However, it seems apparent that if there had been greater social acceptance of gender variance, Marlow would be a boy who liked flowery clothes and long hair. His style of behavior would not determine his gender, only his gender presentation. However, social pressure is powerful and pervasive. You encounter it when walking down the street, at school, at the grocery store, at church. It is everywhere you go. In Marlow's case, the only way he could be himself was to be seen as a girl. Will Marla always feel that she is a girl? What will happen at puberty? It is impossible to know how Marla will turn out. But the family is clear that having an alive and happy child is worth living with these unknowns.

Gender Expression or Gender Identity?

Some transgender-identified teenagers have never been exposed to the natural expression of gender variance common within gay communities. Thus, they may never have seen gender expression that matches their own natural inclinations reflected in another person of their sex. In other words, your child may not be transgender, per se, but may have a natural desire to express their gender in a more cross-gender manner. Their (inner) gender identity may stay aligned with their biological sex, whereas their (outer) expression of gender may not.

I didn't know that women could look like men and still feel like women. I went to Seattle and saw two gay men holding hands. I was blown away, as I had never seen gay people in public before. Just before I stopped staring, they turned toward me and I saw that

*they weren't men at all, they were two women who looked like men
holding hands. These were lesbians. I didn't take in so much that
they were lesbians, my heart just jumped and I said to myself
"that's me!" I had been struggling with thinking I was transgender.
In that flash of seeing women dressed in the clothes that I like, with
boxers on, loose jeans, men's shirts, short hair, and walking in that
way I thought only guys did, I realized that I wasn't a guy at all. I
was one of them. My whole world changed that day. I don't know
if I'm a lesbian or not, but I do know that I am a woman like those
women are.* —16-year-old female

When parents of newly out transgender teens call Stephanie at Gender Spectrum, one of the first things she asks is if their children have
been exposed to significantly gender-variant adults of the same sex as
their child. In other words, if a male child has met and spent time with
feminine men or transwomen, or if a female child has met and spent
time with more masculine women or transmen. If this is not the case,
she suggests that they promptly get their child connected with some
adults who are gender-variant, as well as different types of gay and lesbian folk. Just meeting one gender-variant person, trans person, or gay
person may not be enough—one person does not represent a wide
enough breadth of experience, identity, or presentation. Parents and
caregivers should also find other teenagers as part of this representa-
tion. All of this may require making contact with the closest metropolitan area's gay community center, or an LGBT resource center that is
part of a college or university. It could mean contacting the local chapter of PFLAG or a gay–straight alliance for suggestions. Families might
want to attend a gathering like the annual Gender Spectrum Youth and
Family Conference so they can meet other teens and adults who find
themselves all across the gender spectrum.

When a child is only exposed to a limited range of gender expression, they may feel that they don't belong to that gender. It is critical for

your child to understand which part of their core identity does not feel right. This is tricky: they have to figure out if their gender identity, their gender presentation/expression, or their sexual orientation is the issue, or if it is a combination. Allow your teen the opportunity to meet gender-variant adults—seeing reflections of themselves in others will help them clarify who they are. If you cannot find people within your own communities (or even if you can), suggest watching movies that reflect different parts of the LGBTQ spectrum.

If your teen expresses that they are transgender, they may very well be. But it may stem from an inaccurate assessment of which part of their core self is coming into being. Providing this opportunity for clarity, while still supporting them in this process of self-discovery, will be one of the greatest gifts you can give your child. You, too, will be able to rest more comfortably knowing that your child is not making this decision on a whim, or in reaction to a negative experience. If they continue to feel they are transgender after being exposed to many forms of variance, then they probably are.

Because of the complexity of adolescence, it is not always apparent what is going on. If your child thinks they may be transgender, it's best to make sure they have a supportive, educated counselor to help them distinguish what is true for them. However, be aware that most therapists are not familiar with gender identity issues and may pressure a teen to identify as gay rather than transgender, because it is more socially acceptable. Make sure that you find a therapist who has both an open mind and training in transgender issues.

Don't Push Your Child into a Transgender Identity

Currently there is an emerging group of biological male children who are living transgender lives due to the nonconformity of their social gender. To date, we are not aware of biological female children who are living a transgender life due to the pressures put on them for their gender expression. It is more common to know girls with short hair, or who particularly like rougher sports such as football, or prefer wearing baggy skater shorts rather than skirts. These girls are socially accepted or tolerated as tomboys and are not viewed as particularly gender-variant. However, this freedom of gender expression is not afforded to girls in all communities. The pressure to live a cross-gender life due to narrow social norms is something that many families with gender-variant children must confront.

It is not appropriate to choose a child's gender identity for them for the purpose of your own comfort. Please seek counseling, if needed, to manage your personal discomfort with your child's fluidity of expression and preferences. Living a transgender life is not something a parent should ever push a child into. Nor is it something to be feared if it is the life your child lives. A transgender life is, however, a different life from that of a gender-fluid boy who loves to express his femininity or a gender-fluid girl who loves to express her masculinity.

Could This Just Be a Phase?

For some children, expressing gender variance may be a phase; for others, it is not. The longer a child has identified as cross-gender, the easier it becomes for a parent to answer this question. Regardless of the eventual outcome, the self-esteem, mental well-being, and overall health of a gender-variant child relies heavily on receiving love, support, and compassion from their parents.

With children whose gender-variant identity has remained stable and unchanged, parents can expect that this will most likely continue and only deepen throughout the child's lifetime. For example, a 12-year-old child who has consistently asserted that he is a girl since the age of 3 will most likely remain cross-gender throughout life.

On the other hand, a very young child who feels cross-gender may later change their mind. This occurs infrequently, but usually before puberty; the most common time is around 9–10 years old. There is insufficient research to know if these children later identify as gender-variant or transgender adults. So it is unclear whether this change indicates sublimation or if the cross-gender expression was just a childhood phase.

Sexual Orientation

Gender variance may or may not be an indicator of a child's later sexual orientation. Gender variance and sexual orientation are separate elements that are often interwoven. Sexual orientation, the third component of core identity, refers to the persons to whom we are attracted, romantically or sexually. Gender variance refers to gender-typed behaviors/interests that fit outside what is considered normal for a person's assigned biological sex.

A higher percentage of gender-variant children than nongender-variant children will grow up to be gay. However, gender variance is not a marker of sexual orientation: plenty of gender-variant children do not grow up to be gay, and plenty of children who are not gender-variant become gay.

Studies show, resolutely, that sexual orientation is not a choice. Absolutely nothing a parent or anyone else does will cause a child to be gay or prevent a child from being gay. Sexual orientation is an inherent part of a person's core identity. Unfortunately, many people do not realize this; there is much misinformation about sexual orientation. As a result, caregivers use parenting practices that, while well-intended, may make children and teens who are gay or struggling with their sexual identity feel very bad about themselves. Research from the Family Acceptance Project indicates that family support can decrease the negative impact of parental rejection on attempted suicide in gay, lesbian, and bisexual young people. In fact, the same body of research indicates that even a small increase in family acceptance and support related to their child's LGB identity can have an important impact on their child's health and well-being.

Strong parenting practices that enhance a child's self-esteem are central to good parenting. If you are raising a child who is gender-nonconforming, this becomes especially crucial. Throughout this book, we discuss concrete parenting tools and techniques that you can employ to support your gender-variant or transgender child. As documented by the Family Acceptance Project research, your responses to your children and the support—or lack of support—that you show them have a greater impact on their future outlook on life than any other factor.

Sexual orientation is believed to be established in childhood, and most children seem to be aware of same-sex attraction by around age 10. However, they often don't share this information with anyone for another year or more, since they are still figuring out what it means. They may also wait to disclose this realization to their parents based on how accepting they feel their families may be.

Coming to Terms with Sexual Orientation Variance as a Way to Accept Gender Variance

Accepting sexual orientation as a core part of everyone's identity is a critical component of accepting gender variance. This is not because every gender-variant child will be gay—they won't. It is because homophobia is based on the perception that someone might be gay. And in childhood, that perception is based on a child's behaviors, expressions, or preferences that are not considered typical for the child's anatomical sex. Thus, most gender-variant children and teens are the victims of homophobia—regardless of their actual or future sexual orientation.

Gender-variant children as young as 3 years old suffer from homophobia, often on a daily basis. The rejection, ridicule, and pressure to conform to expected gender norms intensify as children age. The message given to gender-variant children is expressed in different ways, but often boils down to this: the way they are, and who they are, is not good enough.

One of the ways to most effectively support gender-nonconforming children is to resist homophobia. By doing so you accept the possibility that your child may be gay, and help them feel good about themselves. By eliminating exposure to homophobia, and addressing it when you come across it, you help gender-variant children grow up in environments where discrimination is not tolerated.

One of the most concrete ways to make room for gender-variant children, teens, and the gender-variant adults they may grow up to be is to carefully examine the messages of homophobia we provide children, and put an end to them. This is an anti-bias and antibigotry issue. Indeed, hate crimes and hate language are against the law. Yet in our own homes, churches, and communities homophobia is rampant. By putting an end to homophobia, we can make more room for the natural expression of gender-variant children whether or not they are gay or lesbian. This is an issue that can save lives—possibly your own child's life.

Examining Your Own Homophobia

Many people have already examined their own attitudes and decided to live and let live. However, we have all been instructed in the gender system and our reaction to "gay" expression in children can trigger some unexpected reactions. It can be very painful to witness in yourself or others the gut fear and repulsion of parents for their own child. This unbidden response comes to parents who never even considered themselves homophobic. This is not your fault. The gender training we have all been exposed to from the day we were born includes not only exalting the value of heterosexuality, but also interlinking the values of the ideal male with heterosexuality. Thus, the message communicated to all of us, but especially to males, is that perceived or actual homosexuality is an affront to true masculinity. This message is often stronger in certain ethnic and religious communities.

The idea that perceived or actual homosexuality is an affront to true masculinity is so strong, in fact, that a son who is significantly gender-variant can make a father feel that he can't even be around his own son. Some fathers become literally nauseated to witness their son's natural interests, how he prefers to dress, how he naturally walks. It can be horrifying to realize that you feel this way about your own child. Have compassion for yourself if your initial reaction to your gender-variant child is repulsion. We discuss this reaction, and some ways to work through it, in upcoming chapters. Know that you are not alone in reacting like this, however unbidden, unwanted, and surprising it may be.

It is a studied phenomenon that parents subconsciously consider their children to be extensions of themselves. Within this framework, a male child who is gender-variant (and thus perceived as gay) threatens the masculinity of his father. What often happens is that the father blames the mother for somehow causing this. The poison of homophobia within the gender system spreads to the whole family constellation.

For some, the value of heterosexuality is central to strictly held religious and cultural beliefs. Thus, accepting that some people are gay or lesbian runs counter to the foundations of their belief system. Many of you reading this book will deal with this issue head-on: how to accept your child while maintaining your relationship with your religious community. Rather than present an argument about religion, or dissect specific religious practices, we will cut directly to the chase. Many families we know have decided to switch to a welcoming church (several mentioned the United Church of Christ, Unitarian Church, and the Metropolitan Community Church), a progressive synagogue, or another spiritual practice altogether, and felt such relief in doing so. So if you are experiencing stress about how to reconcile your religious beliefs with your instinctual love for your child, you may have a choice to make. We will discuss this further in Chapter 4, Start Where You Are: Moving from Damaging to Effective Parenting Practices. You can do further research online; visit www.religioustolerance.org.

Is Being Gay Ever a Phase?

For most people, being gay or lesbian is not a phase. Rather, it is a core part of who they are. However, some teens in the process of discovering their gender identity may experience confusion as they struggle to understand their sexual orientation. A preteen or teen may believe they are gay for a while, and then, over time, realize they are not gay but actually transgender. So for some transgender teens, being gay is indeed a phase. This is something that will reveal itself as the teen matures.

Some Children or Teens May Mistakenly Think They Are Transgender

Some children have been raised with so much homophobia and such strict gender training that instead of acknowledging their romantic attraction for the same sex, they assume they must really be transgender. They feel that there is no way they could ever be gay—it isn't possible, it wouldn't be right. However, if they were actually transgender, it might all make sense. Instead of being gay and experiencing same-sex attraction, their attraction would be for the "opposite" sex. As outlandish as this rationalization may seem, it can form in the mind of a child who wants to continue being loved and accepted by their family and community. Once again, seeing a therapist familiar with both sexual orientation and gender identity can help your child clarify what part of identity needs to come forth. Likewise, attending a conference with people all across the gender spectrum can also help with this process.

If My Kid Is Transgender, Could They Also Be Gay?

Transgender people have as wide a range of sexual orientations as any other people. Some trans people are straight, some are gay, and some are bisexual. This gets confusing, because we are taught to understand how people interact with one another based on their anatomical sex.

I can accept that my son feels he's a girl. It's taken a long time, but I think I get it. But if he then marries a man, I don't see how you can tell me he's not gay. I just don't get it. I mean if he has sex reassignment surgery then obviously he's not gay anymore, but if he doesn't then he's gay. Of course, if he falls in love with a girl then everyone will think he's a lesbian, anyway, since he lives life full-time as a woman. —Parent of a 20-year-old transwoman

I realized at the age of 3 that I was transgender. Everything inside myself is male and I have thought and felt that way as long as I can remember. Now I identify as a trans straight man. —16-year-old transboy

Of course, when one person is transgender, conversation and negotiation are required for dating and sexual relations. That is a separate issue that we cover briefly in the section on the teen years in Chapter 3, Developmental Stages and the Transgender Child.

If My Child Is Really Transgender, What Should I Do?
First, take a deep breath. Take your time. Listen to your child. Find support for yourself and your family. Read this book, and other materials you may find. Because this is an emerging field, there may not be local professionals trained yet in your area. Your best avenues of support may initially be online.

Kids who are gender-variant and transgender need a lot of support. So do their parents, their siblings, and their extended family members. We will help you proceed through the stages of acceptance and good parenting practices in the following chapters.

Chapter 2

Family Acceptance:
From Crisis to Empowerment

COMING TO TERMS with your child's gender identity and expression—whether because your child announces one day that they are transgender, or by watching your young child unfold to become a transgender or significantly gender-variant person—can often trigger a protracted parental crisis.

Parents' emotional responses in realizing their child is significantly gender-variant or transgender vary from parent to parent, and family to family. Initially most parents feel that their world is falling apart. There is a profound sense of devastation, loss, shock, confusion, anger, fear, shame, and grief. This personal, internal crisis, for some, can take years to resolve. Not all the responses described below pertain to every parent, but we imagine that you will find yourself reflected here.

The initial emotional responses are typically marked by a struggle to comprehend what is going on with your child, and how to convey it to others. For most families there is a natural phase of concealment before acceptance. At the same time as the internal personal revolution is occurring, most parents are searching for information to understand what their child is experiencing and how best to respond to it. In the best cases, parents try to support their child, conceal their internal upheaval, and struggle to adjust, all simultaneously.

Over time, through hard emotional work and dedication to their children, parents can gain a new perspective on gender, and naturally move toward greater acceptance of their child. Some people feel acceptance as a complete shift that occurs inside themselves. For others it is a natural process that occurs over time and often coincides-with the realization that to do anything but accept their child is adding to the stress and distress their child experiences. But coming to true acceptance of your gender-variant or transgender child usually takes a few years.

Fathers' Responses

Often fathers have the hardest time accepting their gender-variant or transgender children. Many fathers pressure their children to conform under the threat of violence or shame. Sometimes, physical abuse occurs. Fathers report feeling embarrassed by their children and being uncomfortable around them. They often blame their child's mother.

Now, obviously, not all fathers react this way. But the majority of fathers we have seen present this kind of initial response to gender variance in their children. Over time, and with deepening understanding, all parents can come to respect and support their children. Fathers do not intend to hurt their children by their initial responses; they usually believe that they are simply "not encouraging them."

We discuss some of the research on parenting and gender variance in chapter 4, Start Where You Are. There you will see that well-meaning parenting practices can actually increase the risks children face as gender-variant and transgender youth.

Conflict within the Family

Parents often blame the other parent for the gender variance. The roles established for which parent is more accepting and which is more cautious are in some cases rigid, and sometimes they rotate between parents. This seems to be true whether parents live together or in separate homes. Most parents feel as if their life is slipping down a slippery slope when they realize that their child is transgender or significantly gender-variant. This parental emotional crisis can serve to destabilize the family unit at just the time when the child needs the most family support.

Given long-held beliefs about gender and immense pressure from society, it is easy to understand why conflict commonly occurs among family members when faced with a child or teen who is significantly gender-nonconforming or transgender. Parents do not reach understanding and acceptance of gender variance overnight, and they may experience considerable stress while coming to terms with their child's gender variance. Each parent must take the time they need to come to acceptance. When there is a disparity in the progress of acceptance between the parents, it can naturally increase the stress in the family. It is normal to feel uncomfortable, embarrassed, angry, devastated, nervous, or afraid during this time. It is normal to feel desperate to find and grasp "solid" answers. Parental discomfort affects the entire family. Sometimes this causes serious ruptures in family equilibrium. Depending on the family and the situation, it may take months or years for harmony to return.

We hope that despite the misgivings you may feel, you are able to separate them from your job as a parent. In other words, it is completely fine to feel bewildered, angry, sad, and disheartened—these feelings will change over time, but they need to be felt. Remember that you are still a parent and that your child-rearing does not wait for you to catch up emotionally. It remains your job to create a home full of love, support, safety, and nurturance. We hope that the research provided later in the book will be useful in guiding you to make healthy parenting choices for your child while you progress through your own adjustment period.

Acceptance Takes Time

> *I feel I am seeing my child clearly now. I feel I have been given a unique and great person who is changing me like no one else ever will. I love all my kids so much and I am so impressed at the love and bonds that have been made because there is an issue that we all share and all take a part of.* —Parent of a 7-year-old transboy

It is essential for parents and other family members to realize that acceptance is not a linear process. It is slow, and it takes time. It also takes dedication, resolve, and effort. It is very important for the future of your relationship with your child that you do not stop your growth process at partial acceptance. Continue to be open to growing, step by step, until you reach true acceptance. It is only at that point that your life will again feel harmonious and balanced. Balance comes when the issue of your child's gender is no longer foremost in your mind, but is simply a small part of who your child is.

Acceptance is a progression; it is always a matter of degrees. It rests on multiple factors including personal beliefs, political beliefs, and religious beliefs. Acceptance is easier for those who already value diversity. For those who value conformity, it is much more difficult to come to true acceptance. However, each step toward acceptance is vital and none should be undervalued. There is no established timeline for true acceptance of your child. But perseverance and personal dedication to coming to terms will serve you well.

When You Already Have an Understanding of Gender Variance

Some parents are more open to or are already familiar with the idea of gender variance. Maybe they have a transgender co-worker, or they are lesbian or gay parents, or live in a more liberal enclave with a visible LGBT community, or are simply part of a more fluid group of gender-variant friends. Such parents may be able to cope more easily with the fact of their child's gender variance and can skip parts of what, for most, is a huge personal crisis. These parents may focus more on their fear for their child's current and future safety. However, while greater comfort with gender variance or a personal experience with it can mitigate the depth of the crisis, there is still a natural adjustment period that involves a good deal of personal questioning and exploration. It should be noted that lesbian and gay parents do not necessarily feel more at ease raising a gender-variant or transgender child. In fact, lesbian and gay parents, who are often under so much self-inflicted pressure to be "perfect," may be even more shocked to realize that their child's gender is beyond their control. Not only that, lesbian and gay parents are frequently accused of "causing" their child to be transgender or gender-variant, and they must be explicitly prepared for such comments.

Fear for the Safety and Well-being of Your Child

I'm a bit more protective of my child these days. I hesitate to have other kids over anymore, unless I really know them, since some of them have made fun of him once they see his girl stuff. I also worry about his future, as I know how cruel folks can be, and I worry for his safety. —Parent of a 6-year-old gender-variant boy

As a parent of course you have to think of your kid's safety, and I try not to think about this too much. But there have been the horror stories about people being hurt or worse by the bigots that are out there. I just pray that the world will start becoming more educated on this whole issue, and with knowledge, my fear will dissipate. —Parent of a 24-year-old transwoman

All parents with gender-variant children express these fears, over and over again: Will my child make friends? Who will love my child? Will my child suffer as the victim of hate crimes? Will my child suffer physical violence? Will my child suffer sexual violence? Will my child commit suicide? Will my child be murdered? Will my child be discriminated against as an adult in terms of jobs and housing?

These fears can feel absolutely debilitating at times. They are one of the root causes of why parents try to change their children. Parents are afraid for their children. Over time, this fear can be successfully mobilized into anger, and the anger can be harnessed to change the world. Go out there and fight for the right of your child, and all children, to be safe.

> *I would like to say to those who do not understand: watch out, I will protect my kid.* —Parent of a 7-year-old transboy

Fear of Condemnation

Parents of gender-variant children do not choose to be scrutinized. They just happen to be raising a gender-variant or transgender child. But, rightly so, many parents fear the responses of others to the discovery of their parenting choices for their gender-variant child. People who know nothing of your child's truth can be very judgmental. And it can be scary not to know if you will be shunned from your important communities because of this. What often results is an internalization of shame—a feeling that you have done something wrong as a parent to transgress understood rules or codes of behavior.

> *We were really afraid that our friends or neighbors would call Child Protective Services if we allowed our child to change pronouns. We were really afraid that someone would try to take our child away for the very act of supporting him. We finally decided that in order to change his pronoun, as he so desperately needed us to do, we had to find a well-respected therapist who would support our parenting choices, if need be. And mind you, we live in Berkeley. I can't imagine the guts it takes to support your transgender child in Iowa!* —Parents of 5-year-old transboy

This fear of the judgment of others can lead to the very awkward and uncomfortable feeling of being embarrassed about your child, especially in public. These feelings of shame and embarrassment often get folded into that "protecting my child" feeling. In other words, many parents don't want to admit that their child is embarrassing to them in public. They don't want to admit that they are afraid of other people's perceptions of them and their child. So they tell themselves, *I think he'd be a lot safer if he didn't wear that dress.* But perhaps the truth is actually this: *I think I'd feel a lot more comfortable if he didn't wear that dress.*

To come to terms with your feelings of shame and embarrassment, it is important first to recognize them for what they are.

Grief

The grief that parents raising gender-variant and transgender children experience falls into two distinct categories. The first is the grief over lost dreams for your child. The second is the grief that parents of transgender children feel for the child who goes away in order for the new one to emerge. Although parents of gender-variant children experience the loss of their dreams, parents of transgender kids also experience the loss of the child they knew.

> But what about my dreams for my child? I feel some sense of loss for the childhood I never got to share with my daughter, and a big hole where I once thought a little boy was. —Parent of a 20-year-old transwoman

Perhaps the most painful part of the process of accepting your child is letting go of the fantasies you held for your child—and also the fantasies of what you were going to share together in the future. Countless mothers of transgender sons have expressed to Stephanie their sadness at letting go of their vision of sharing their daughter's wedding day, and the birth of her first child. They were terribly sad that this would never happen now that they had a son instead of their daughter. Parents face reworking their dreams for their children.

But it may be helpful to remember that all parents must do this to some extent, as their children individuate and take paths different from the ones their parents planned for them. Often parents hope that their children will live out the dreams they never realized in their younger years.

> *I busted my knee in high school. I had been a football player. I knew that any son of mine would be a great football player. One of the hardest things for me about my son saying he was a girl was my dream fading before my eyes. I didn't want to let go of it. I was so mad at him for not liking football.*
>
> *One day I realized that I was punishing him for not being me. I took a good look at him and saw that he was afraid of me; it was getting pretty close to him hating me. He was only 6, but I knew that day that I had a choice to make. Let go of my old dreams that were killing my relationship with my son or lose my son for good.*
>
> *I am still not quite ready to let my son be my daughter. That's a lot to ask. But I am ready to put my love for him ahead of my anger. I pray every day to be a strong enough man to love my son enough to let him be just exactly who he is—even if that means he is really a girl.* —Parent of an 8-year-old gender-variant child

We can't choose our children's personal preferences, or their personal expressions. We cannot choose for them who they are and who they will be. When parents let go of dreams for their child, they often realize that their truest hopes and dreams for their child remain the same. They want their children to be happy, they want them to love and be loved, and they want them to have the joy of family and children. These dreams remain the same whether they are gender-variant, transgender, or typically gendered.

When Your Child Transitions

The term *transition* refers to the time period during which your child outwardly changes gender, as well as to the act of changing genders. Once a family has consented to allowing their child to live in accordance with their gender identity, a number of changes must happen. Often there are name changes, pronoun changes, and personal presentation changes. For some, this is an overnight process, but for most it is a process that takes place over a number of months. If your child is nearing puberty or is already a teen, there are medical decisions to be made about hormone inhibitors, cross-hormones, and possible future surgeries. With young children, this process often happens over a period of years without being consciously felt as a transition. For example, the parents may have allowed their child early on to have a hairstyle more in alignment with their inner gender, or made some clothing changes, as well. The transition is complete when the gender has changed and the use of pronouns has changed.

Emotional Responses to Your Child's Transition

When a child transitions—whether at 4 or at 17, families—parents and siblings alike—may feel a sense of grief at the idea they are "losing" their son or daughter, brother or sister. Even though the child is alive and well, changing gender can elicit strong feelings of loss. In fact, most parents compare it to the death of their child. Their child becomes, in a sense, a new child, but the new child carries the memories and experiences of the previous child.

Grief

Many books on grief document the stages of coming to terms with loss. Families with a child undergoing a gender transition report similar phases of emotional response to the loss. Intense and varying periods of denial, sadness, anger, and mourning are common in dealing with and accepting this new emerging identity. According to people who study grief and loss, you should expect to actively grieve a serious loss for one year. Your grief is made much more difficult because the object of your grief—the child you have lost—is a bit like a phantom: in reality your child is still here and needs your support more than ever. They have not died; rather, they are blossoming into themselves!

This grief is unique, because unlike other forms of loss that are socially recognized and acknowledged, the grief connected with coming to terms with your gender-variant or transgender child is not culturally understood. Not only do others not understand the grief, but the grief can also be confusing to you. Many parents question what right they have to feel as if their child has died when the child is right in front of them.

The grief is compounded by emotional responses already discussed, such as shame. If you are concealing your child's gender variance and are ashamed about your child, you will likely be isolated in your grief. Isolation in grief can spiral easily into depression.

Regret and Self-blame

It breaks my heart when I think of the dark and lonely nights that he spent wondering and worrying how to deal with it all. For nearly 10 years my child traveled down this emotionally painful journey alone. And I, the mother, could not see! —Parent of a 23-year-old transwoman

There is usually a time during the progression to true acceptance of their child when a parent looks back with remorse at some of their past parenting choices. This is natural. If you have other children, remember that you can look back over their lives and feel some regret for parenting choices with them, as well. Be kind to yourself as you look back. We all do the best we can as parents. Most parents feel some guilt about occasions when they didn't listen to their child. Looking back, they realize there had been signs all along. Some parents recall conversations where they dismissed their child outright from talking about their gen-

Unconditional Love

There is no greater possible source of love in your life than your children. Your children base their world upon your love and acceptance of them. Unconditional love can be the key to bringing you back to the present moment. You can use it as a parenting focus: How do I need to grow to allow me to unconditionally love my child, even when my child is not as I expected they would be? What needs to change in me so that my focus can be on helping to smooth the way for my child, to minimize the trauma they experience, to make their life as easy and as joyful as possible?

der variance. Parents also feel remorse over having pushed their child to be more typically gendered. A new and unique form of remorse is now felt by parents who forced their transgender children to be "out" to others rather than allowing them to choose whom they wanted to tell.

Does Anything Make This Personal Crisis Easier?

Come Back to Your Parenting Beliefs

When confronted with a big challenge in your parenting, it helps to return to your philosophical foundation of parenting. These are your bottom-line beliefs about parenting. When you approach your struggles around your child's gender by remembering that love, support, compassion, empathy, and protection of your children are a parent's solemn responsibility, it becomes easier to progress. This technique of remembering your foundational parenting beliefs does not end your personal crisis. Your feelings are yours to have—you must go through them and come out on the other side. But return often to the touchstone of your foundational beliefs to help you focus on moving through the crisis, rather than clinging to old beliefs that are keeping you distant from your child. You may even want to write them down to pull out during particularly painful moments.

Hold Love to Be More Important Than Social Mores and Societal Expectations

Studies of parents of transgender children of all ages have found that the parents who hold love paramount fare best in accepting their gender-variant children. Keep coming back to love as your guide. It can really help you make the right decisions. Parents teach their children to resist peer pressure—it is up to parents to do the same. Parents of gender-variant and transgender children are given repeated opportunities to choose love.

It is hard for parents to be required to face societal prejudice just for loving their child. Although it is a tough move to make, we suggest you try it. Many families with a transgender child have moved from rural areas to more progressive urban areas of the country to find a wider array of individuals with whom they can share their lives fully. Others have chosen to remain in their communities, thereby bringing the important people in their lives along with them on the journey of education, acceptance, and understanding. There will be more discussion of this in Chapter 6, Disclosure: Whom to Tell, How, Why, and When.

Focus on Your Child's Happiness

Parents across the country have reported to Gender Spectrum that when they allow their children and teens to express themselves in the ways that are most natural to them, to live in accordance with their true gender identity, the improvement is amazing. Depressed, anxious, hostile, or withdrawn children become visibly happier. A greater sense of inner peace appears in them.

I didn't know what to do. Our son asked us over and over again to call him she. I just couldn't bring myself to do it. Finally our family therapist asked—is it making him happy for you to insist on calling him a boy? Of course the answer was no. But then when he asked me if it would make my son happy if I called him she—the answer was a clear yes. He then asked me what was more important to me than my child's happiness. That was a tough one. I started to cry. I realized that my fear of ridicule coupled with my fear of the ridicule he would suffer was causing me to deny him true happiness. —Parent of a 12-year-old transgirl

Ongoing Closeness and Connection with Your Child

Strive every day to be close to your child, even in the midst of your anger, confusion, and grief. Remember that parents and children have potential for the most meaningful relationships. But relationships take work and dedication. Keep turning toward your child—look them in the eye. Be courageous, and keep coming back to your love. Try to look at your child with admiration and inquisitiveness. Ask yourself, What is this person bringing me in my life? What is the gift here? Count your blessings with your child.

If you are currently alienated from your child, do not lose hope. Children always are ready to bring their parents back into their lives. They want your love and closeness more than anything. Go toward your child. What do you have to lose? It can be humbling, but it will bring joy and meaning back into your lives.

Meet Other Families with Gender-variant Children

While coming to terms with your child's gender variance is often a difficult path to navigate, it is not one you need travel alone. Support is as critical for parents as it is for the children. Connecting with other families who have a gender-variant child can go miles toward diminishing feelings of isolation and the shame you may be experiencing. You can enlist the help of your local children's hospital in setting up a support group, or you can place flyers with local pediatricians. Although national Listservs are invaluable for many families across the country, nothing compares to actually meeting other children who are transgender, bi-gendered, nongendered, or gender-variant.

Attending a national conference with parents of other gender-variant and transgender children and teens will allow you to make connections, learn about the latest research and pertinent information, and become active in the gender movement. Conferences are one of the most powerful forms of support available to you. Every family should have the experience of being in an environment where their type of family is the norm.

It is crucial for you and your child to meet other transgender and gender-variant people—meet as many as you can. Many transgender persons have suffered the loss of their families in becoming their true selves. Many have the continued love and support of their families. Some transgender people have partial support and acceptance from family members. There are transgender adults who blend into society and therefore suffer little discrimination, while others suffer daily for their self-expression.

There are support groups and conferences for transgender people in every area of the country. Many colleges now commemorate Transgender Day of Remembrance in November and sometimes hold Transweek programming that is open to the public. Through these activities, you will likely meet transgender persons of all ages and types. This is important to you as the parent of a gender-variant child, and it is essential if you suspect or know that your child is transgender. Make the effort, no matter how scary it seems. Ask a friend to go with you.

Some parents are initially concerned that meeting other gender-variant or cross-gender people will somehow rub off on their children and "encourage" them. In truth, gender variance is not contagious. If anything, your child may initially be very shy in such a setting, not believing that there can be others who feel as they do. Over time, knowing that there are other boys who wear skirts or girls who know they are really boys, or kids who do not feel that they are a boy or a girl, will be of great comfort to your child—but it will not make them someone they are not already.

However, just because a person is transgender does not necessarily mean they are someone you would like your child to know. As a parent, you must first reach out and meet transgender adults on your own. Once you have found contacts you would like your child to meet, you can facilitate those connections.

Educate Yourself

Parents coming to terms with their child's gender variance often begin their search by looking for the most basic information. In the process, they learn a whole new way of accessing resources. We have listed current sources of information and support in Chapters 4, 7, 8, and 9. The internal revolution that comes from educating yourself and integrating your personal experience is a transformation that will enrich your life and deepen your respect for diversity in its many forms.

The process of self-education takes many forms as well. Some parents resist learning about gender and the politics of gender, whereas others seem to find personal serenity by reading everything they can on the subject. Finding balance here is important.

Siblings

Because of your discomfort with your child's gender variance, you may unconsciously bond with your other children more than your gender-variant child. By doing this, you inadvertently place the nontransgender sibling in a position of having to choose loyalty to their parent or to their sibling.

My dad always wanted to play with me. It was fun, but it made me feel bad inside because he never asked my brother to play with us and he never said yes to play the games my brother wanted to play. I am so glad he is changing. That was really hard for me. —Terrek, gender-typical sibling, age 10

Feeling Second Best

The reverse is also common; some parents overly focus on the gender-nonconforming child, neglecting the other children as a result. It is easy to spend so much time in the early years stressing about your gender-variant child, learning about gender, processing with friends, and researching gender-related topics that your other children can feel less important.

It can be helpful to read books about the siblings of special-needs children. The library has books written for siblings and parenting books for adults. These resources can provide you with tips for making sure your other children do not grow up feeling second best.

Stress

Our 14-year-old had some challenges at first, but now she is so happy that she has a great little brother. —Parent of a 7-year-old transboy

Some families with gender-variant or transgender children are in a perpetual state of crisis for a number of years. The stress of this affects everyone in the family. Be careful not to overlook the stress exhibited by the other children in the family, and be sure to seek therapy if the stress seems to be turning into distress.

Some families have declared "transfree times." These are times where no one discusses gender for a day, a meal, an outing. It may seem silly to need to declare such time—but the other siblings will be greatly appreciative. This can be a private adult agreement; the kids don't even have to know. When you try this, if you find it is tricky, you know that you have been spending too much family time talking about gender.

Sibling Teasing

Gender-variant children may trigger unwanted teasing and bullying, even from their own siblings. Siblings may participate because they feel pressure from their peers to ostracize or to be critical of their nonconforming sibling. While siblings must be allowed their full range of feelings, you must absolutely place limits on their freedom to ridicule the nonconforming sibling. Every family member is entitled to a ridicule-free space in their own home. Do not tolerate teasing or taunting based on gender identity or gender expression from either siblings or their friends.

Likewise, you should teach siblings to stick up for one another, and provide them with the language for doing so. Tell them to say to teasing friends, "I don't want to play with you if you keep teasing my sister." They might add something like "She is who she is, and I love her."

Sometimes siblings are teased simply because they have a gender-variant or transgender sister or brother. Be sensitive to the impact your child's gender nonconformity has on your other children. Be prepared to support your children in learning skills to resist bullying, and talk to the school on their behalf, if needed.

Sibling Grief

Siblings of transgender children go through a grieving process similar to the grieving process their parents go through. For some siblings, the grief is even stronger than their parents'. The grief can be confusing to the child and can be protracted. This grief can easily turn into depression, so keep an eye on your other children; professional support may be helpful during this time of transition.

When a child is allowed to undertake a gender transition and to outwardly live in accordance with their inner gender identity, they often become more social and outgoing. This can result in new social opportunities that may leave the gender-typical sibling feeling neglected or discarded.

My sister was 3 when she told us she was a boy. I was 11. I was so sad. I was mad at her—why did she need to be a boy? Why couldn't she keep being my sister? I had waited so long for a sister, and now I wouldn't even have one. I refused to call him by his new name for the longest time. Now, of course, I can't imagine him as a girl. That was a long time ago. I don't really think much about the sister I used to have. But when I look at pictures of him when he was still a girl, it makes me sad inside. —Older sister of a trans brother

Telling Others about the Gender-variant Sibling

Word has gotten out and many of the friends of my youngest have questioned him about his sibling. He says this annoys him because he doesn't want to talk about it very often. —Parent of a 20-year-old trans daughter

Siblings may act out in an effort to gain attention, possibly in ways that are hurtful to their gender-variant sibling. For example, the sibling may "out" or disclose personal information about the gender-nonconforming child at inappropriate times or in a disrespectful manner. Although this is a cry for attention, it can backfire by generating negative attention in the form of punishment, a lecture, or alienation from the transgender or gender-variant sibling. If the sibling continues to speak inappropriately to others, try to ascertain what is going on underneath. Your child is probably trying to tell you something; take the time to listen. They probably need reassurance that they are perfect the way they are, and that they are special, too. Make an effort to spend quality time together and provide gentle, daily reminders of your love. At the same time, make it clear that family members do not disclose private information about others in the family.

In some families, the transgender child prefers to keep parts of their gender expression or identity private. Depending on the age of the siblings involved, it can be difficult for them to grasp the significance of this need for privacy. Children like to share about their lives with their friends. There is a fine line between privacy and secrecy, and parents need to help everyone learn the difference.

Give your children every opportunity to discuss their questions and concerns about the gender-variant sibling. Help them with the language needed to talk about their sibling in a way that feels natural. If you have a transgender child who is not "out," the whole family should discuss how this situation is going to be handled. How does the sibling answer to her friends about what happened to her sister? Why is she dressed that way? Who is this brother they never knew about? How do they refer to the past without mentioning the former gender of their sibling, if it has changed? This is difficult enough for adults to navigate; for children it can be even more trying.

If the child is not transgender but multigender or gender-variant in other ways, it is essential to clarify what part of the gender-variant sibling's personal life, if any, is to remain private. In this respect the need for privacy is no different from issues of privacy between siblings of any kind.

Parental Empowerment

There comes a time in the process of coming to terms with your child's gender expression or gender identity when you finally leave the crisis behind and experience a sense of empowerment. For some, it is a moment they will always remember. But for most, it is a gradual realization that they feel comfortable with their lives again. They feel equipped to handle the challenges of raising their child. There is a greater sense of inner peace.

Living at the Intersection of the Transgender World and the Gender-typical World

For parents and children alike, there is no escape from a gender-rigid culture. Gender is everywhere. Fully accepting your child may require that you change aspects of your personal environment. There is even greater potential for personal loss as you feel the need to search for friends and communities that embrace your children and your parenting choices with kindness and respect. Parents of gender-nonconforming children must seek out the small group of people who understand their children and their parenting choices, against the backdrop of a mainstream culture that does not.

True Acceptance

As a mother, I will do my part to pave the way to a better world for my daughter and for all of the others like her. This means talking openly with others, and not trying to hide our kid. It means becoming politically active in trying to push through legislation in my own state that seeks to end gender discrimination. It means trying to find speaking venues where education can take place. My daughter knows she can count on her mother to shed light on the truth, educate others, and work to make the world a better place, one person at a time. I see this now very clearly. —Mother of a 19-year-old transwoman

True acceptance of a transgender or gender-variant child appears as a range of qualities that, combined, lead to a feeling of balance and a reestablished sense of equilibrium in the family. It is marked by a feeling of having established some form of social support for your parenting choices—by meeting others online, forming a support group, or finding respectful health care professionals to care for your child.

True acceptance is also marked by an understanding of the difference between secrecy and privacy—the ability to feel comfortable knowing when and with whom to disclose information about your child's gender variance, and when it is simply unnecessary. This is something that we will explore more fully in the following chapters.

True acceptance is marked by an understanding of the complexity of gender. This understanding blends your own family experience with the greater system of compulsory gender in our society. It embraces a deeper understanding of the injustices of both homophobia and transphobia. With this enriched understanding of gender comes a transformation in how one sees the world, and parents usually become engaged in gender activism as a result.

Parents approach the idea of gender activism in different ways. Some write, some communicate differently with friends and family, some question the business forms used in their workplace, some engage in educational reform, and others dedicate their lives to gender activism. But there is a natural overflow into your daily life when you realize that there is nothing wrong with your child. If the problem lies with the system, you work to change the system that discriminates against your child.

Lastly, but most significantly, true acceptance is reached when you can have a positive outlook for the future of your child and fear no longer dominates that view. When you can imagine your child as an adult, happy and well loved, you know you have reached parental empowerment.

Chapter 3

Developmental Stages and the Transgender Child

IF YOU'RE A PARENT or caregiver of a gender-variant or transgender child, you've no doubt been frustrated by the lack of information about gender development in most parenting and child-care literature. Here, we present a chapter on the age-specific milestones that pertain specifically to gender development, and the typical ages at which transgender children become self-aware. Of course, as with all developmental stages, this will vary from child to child. We hope that what you read below picks up where the other books leave off.

Ages and Stages

Age 2–3

Gender identity emerges by age 2 to 3 and is influenced by biology and sociological factors. Even before then, babies can identify people by gender presentation and voice recognition. Toddlers quickly learn from both adults and peers the "gender" of toys and certain clothes, and may turn away from or chastise others who cross the gender divide. Once a child has established an internal sense of gender, they actively seek out same-sex models and other cues for learning how to act. This process is the same for children whose gender identity does not match their genitalia. They actively strive to socialize themselves according to their inner sense of gender.

Two-to-three-year-olds want to order their worlds. By this age many children can identify men and women and boys and girls based on external appearances. They are often confused by gender-variant adults and tend to label them as men or women based on basic features such as hair length. By this age, some children have already begun to announce to parents and caretakers that they sense a keen difference between what they are told they are and what they know about their own gender identity. Amazingly, a transgender identity is often very clear by this age.

Age 3–4

By age 3 to 4 children have a sense of their own gender identity and are increasingly aware of anatomical differences. Since their own basic gender identity has been established, they are motivated to learn about the sexes and incorporate this information into gender schemes—organized sets of beliefs and expectations about male and female gender roles. At this age, gender roles are becoming refined through interaction with others, and stereotypes begin to emerge. These stereotypes are self-regulated and based on what children have been exposed to by the media, family values, and social interactions. Gender segregation usually starts at this age and only intensifies until age 12.

Many gender-variant and transgender children at this young age of 3 or 4 are struggling with language to express their differences: "I feel like a boy." "I want to be a girl when I grow up." "I am a girl." "I wish I was a girl." "I wish I was a boy." "God made a mistake with me." "I am half boy and half girl." "My heart is boy, but my body is girl." This is an age at which some parents of gender-variant children are trying to ascertain if this is gender variance or truly a transgender identity. Other parents are still fairly unaware of their child's gender variance.

Age 4–6

Four-to-six-year-olds associate gender with specific behaviors. They are using gender scripts. Girls wear makeup—so anyone with makeup on is a girl. Boys lift weights and play with trucks—so anyone lifting weights or driving a truck is a boy. Even when they see people of the so-called opposite sex engaged in these behaviors, they still think of these behaviors as applying to only one gender or the other. Though a child's mother may be a doctor, at age 4 the child still says that all doctors are men. However, early childhood research shows that when 4-to-6-year-olds are given enough examples through books, storytelling, or repeated exposure to real persons, they can adapt their constructs. School has a great influence on children at this age, so it is essential that preschools and grade schools incorporate gender differences and tolerance of such differences into their programs. By this age, indicators of gender variance clearly emerge in many children—boys play dress-up repeatedly, often fashioning dresses out of whatever they can find (tablecloths, towels, Mother's T-shirts) and girls start refusing more feminine clothing, including feminine underwear and bathing suits.

It is normal for 4-to-6-year-olds to think they can grow up and become the opposite sex, or a hedgehog, or a mermaid. Some children understand gender stability by 5, whereas many others don't fully comprehend it until they are around 7. By this age, many transgender children have been consistent and persistent in their cross-gender identity for several years. It starts to become glaringly apparent that this is not a stage.

Age 5–7

By age 5 to 7 children have an understanding of gender consistency and stability. They understand that one's gender is not going to change: a man is a man even if he dresses like a woman. Once this idea has stabilized, the attachment to stereotypical behaviors subsides and a fuller expression of self and fuller expression of gender is possible. For example, even among nongender-variant kids, girls this age may adamantly declare that they don't like dresses or anything pink anymore, and gravitate toward athletic clothing in hues of green or navy blue. Once established, gender identity is generally fixed for life, though depending on their environment some children may choose not to express their true gender identity until a later time.

Young children believe they can be anything and do anything. But gender stereotypes and roles limit their dreams and experiences. If a child enjoys doing something that is different from the norm, the child might feel embarrassed or uncomfortable because others signal to them that this is wrong. If a child is significantly gender-variant or transgender and is forced to limit their expression at school or in other arenas, it is very typical for them to develop behavioral problems at school, and they may even begin to express suicidal ideation.

Pubertal Changes

Age 9–12

Between ages 9 and 12, a child's gender identity continues to stabilize. In these "tween" years it is common for a subset of the children who have been expressing gender variance throughout childhood to reject this form of self-expression now. Many parents say that it is during these years that their child's gender variance is no longer an issue. Gender-variant boys may cut their hair and start to wear more typically male clothing. They may give away their dolls or sewing things and take up more typically male interests. Likewise, previously solidly gender-variant girls may now retire some of their more masculine clothes and choose to grow their hair out. They may start enacting more stereotypically female behaviors that they had dismissed a year before.

Conversely, at this age, as the pubertal changes begin, underlying gender dysphoria can even more strongly emerge in some children. This may be the time when the family finally recognizes that their child is actually transgender.

Of course, it is common for children to resist the body changes of puberty. For some it represents the end of childhood; for others it is simply odd to feel their body changing. Some feel discomfort at the budding of a sexuality they are not ready to embrace. However, for a child who is transgender, these changes can be a harbinger of depression, self-neglect, and self-destructive behaviors. Such reactions may indicate that your child is experiencing gender-related stress and may even be transgender. Some children of this age realize on their own that they are transgender, whereas others need therapeutic guidance to determine the cause or causes of their inner turmoil.

Our daughter hated getting breasts. She started to wrap them tightly and to wear many layers of undershirts under her baggy overshirts. She cut her hair very short. She wore baggy pants. Everyone thought she was a boy. We just thought she was a tomboy. But when she got her period two things happened that showed us something was very wrong. The first was that she got very depressed. She wouldn't come out of her room—wouldn't talk to us. It was really scary. The second thing that worried us was that when she had her period, she acted as if she didn't have it. She would not use any feminine products. That was so weird we took her to the doctor. At first none of us knew what was going on. But over the next six months we all realized that she was transgender. It was a hard way to lose my daughter. But the son that we have is not depressed. —Parent of a 15-year-old transboy

Age 12–18

During puberty and early adulthood, gender identity generally becomes fully developed. In fact, the third-most-common time for a child to realize they are transgender (after toddlerhood and prepubescence) is during adolescence. For this is when the hormonal and concurrent physical changes of puberty clarify for the child that they are going through the "wrong" puberty. For teenagers this may emerge first as a serious social withdrawal and depression that later develops into a transgender identity. The urgency of their communications at this age reflects less the need to be dramatic and more the fear of the rapidly changing body that is taking them further away from their true nature as the days pass.

> *Increasingly I felt that something was wrong with me. I didn't know what it was. It seemed to get much worse whenever I was in the locker room changing for gym. Somehow being around all those girls made me feel horrible about myself. I started to dread P.E. even though I am a great athlete. I started to cut gym class. Finally my coach told me I wouldn't be able to play basketball if I kept it up. I responded to this by not going to school. My parents didn't know. When they found out they were really worried. I had been an honor roll athlete type all of my life.*
>
> *They sent me to therapy. Over the next few months my therapist and I began to think I was a lesbian. But somehow it just didn't fit. It helped for a few months, but then the depression was back. Finally we started to explore my gender. I was completely freaked out. I totally felt like a guy. I had always felt like a guy. But there was no way I was going to be one of those weird transgender people.*
>
> *My therapist helped me to understand that I was not weird. He explained that it is other people who just don't understand. He explained that some people are transgender and it is normal. He told me there have always been transgender people. He told*

me they were not perverts. I was really scared to talk to my parents about it. Finally my therapist and I did it together.

I am so much happier now living as a boy. I know that the problems just come from lack of understanding. I wish everyone could just be educated about all the possibilities rather than being told you are a girl or a boy. I almost threw my whole life away— just because no one had ever told me that being transgender was a normal possibility.

If I could change one thing, it would be that all people were required to understand that there are more than two categories of gender. That way other kids won't have to suffer like I did.
—17-year-old transboy

Social Anxiety

All too many transgender teens are afraid of going out with friends at all, let alone dating. It does not have to be this way. This response usually comes from a combination of internalized shame about who they are and a lack of full support from their parents. If your child is reclusive it is a good idea to get them help from a trained therapist, and possibly to seek family counseling. Likewise, it is important for you to help your teen make contact with other transgender teenagers so they can see they are not alone. The Internet is the primary way for teens to connect with one another—but it cannot replace valuable in-person relationships.

Crushes and Dating

I don't have a problem dating. I've had lots of girlfriends. But I NEVER date girls from my school. —15-year-old transboy

I date. Sure, I date. But I am very careful. I get to know someone first. I always tell them first. Now everyone at my school knows, but I tell them anyway to see how they react to my face. Some of the guys I date are gay. They feel better about dating me because I am a girl with boy parts. I am not gay. But I end up with a lot of gay guys. —17-year-old transgirl

I can't imagine ever dating. No one at my school knows. What if the girl I wanted to date didn't understand and went and told everyone? It's not worth it, I'm going to wait. —16-year-old transboy

A lot of parents are very nervous about the prospect of their gender-variant or transgender teen developing crushes or dating. Some parents go so far as to ban their children from dating. Although this response is certainly understandable, it is based in fear. It's not a healthy way to approach your child's normal and age-appropriate developmental striving for romance, dating, sexual feelings, and finding a partner. We strongly encourage you to allow your child to date, but you will need to educate them about responsible dating and safe sex.

Most cross-gender children are already nervous about dating. If they are not open about their transgender status, they do not see any possible way they could date. They are afraid of two things—rejection and being outed. And these are very real concerns. Dating and sexual exploration are a normal part of the teenage years for many cross-gender teens. So, as with all things in parenting, it is most helpful to be proactive and to figure out how to best support your child through these times.

You and your child may be surprised by the positive reactions of teens to dating transgender teens. The most common response can be summarized by an eighth-grade student who said: "When you are hot, you're hot! Who cares what is in your pants!"

While other teens may be open to dating your child, we do not recommend that your teen ever get into a situation where their date could potentially discover this information by surprise. For example, this could easily happen through many types of sexual intimacy. The danger comes from the date being completely unprepared for such a discovery and reacting in an impulsive or physically threatening way. Your teen should not engage in any sexual activity with someone who is not aware of their transgender status, as a necessary means of self-protection.

This is very important for you to discuss with your teen. Sexually inexperienced teens do not realize the various ways this could come up. They may think they are safe if they are just kissing—many sexually inexperienced teens do not know that kissing often leads to roaming hands. They may think that darkness will hide their anatomy. To an adult these are obvious misperceptions, but they are not so obvious to an inexperienced teen. Furthermore, many transmale teens—anatomical female teens who identify as male—do not realize that they can get pregnant by having intercourse, because they do not think of themselves as female.

Because there is an increased likelihood of self-deprecation, body shame, and body hatred for transgender teens, it is essential to have sensitive conversations about sex with your teen. Transgender teenagers who have been rejected by their parents or caregivers have a much greater chance of engaging in risky sexual behaviors than those from families with low or no rejection. Transgender teenagers need to be taught about safer sex precautions. This can be an emotionally loaded conversation for your teen, who may reject their sexual anatomy because it doesn't feel as though this anatomy is theirs. Take the time to instruct them about the need for protection. You can do this most effectively by using gender-neutral words to describe their anatomy. For example: "If you choose to have intercourse of any kind, you have to use a condom in order to be safe." "Diseases can be communicated by anal and genital contact, so please make sure you use a dental dam or a condom if your body will have any penetration by others, or if you will be orally pleasuring your sexual partner."

If you cannot bring yourself to have these conversations with your child, we understand. Also, many teens cannot hear this kind of information from their parents. If this is the case, you must find others who can provide this information. This is a concrete way you can help keep your child safe. Take the time to contact the nearest LGBT center, transgender organization, or sexual education center and ask for referrals. Keep searching until you find someone. Planned Parenthood often has very good educators, but you will need to prescreen them to make sure they have information about transgender sexual health. Some organizations provide transgender mentors for trans teens who are able to share information on sex and sexuality when parents cannot.

Sexual Orientation of Your Transgender Teen

Transgender teens and parents of transgender teens alike can be confused about the differences and overlap between sexual orientation and gender identity. A transgender person can have any sexual orientation. If your child identifies as male and is attracted to females, he is straight. This is true even though your son is anatomically female. Conversely, if your son prefers to date boys, he is gay, even though he is anatomically female. If you are focusing on your child's anatomy, this can become confusing. Remember that this is about your child's gender identity, not their anatomical sex. A growing number of gender-variant and transgender teens identify as genderqueer and date within a pool of teens who also have a broad view of gender and sexual orientation.

Even if your child does not identify as gay, lesbian, or genderqueer, sometimes the safest dating pool and support network for them will be the people connected with their local gay–straight alliance. Youth associated with these school clubs are typically more informed and are more accepting of gender diversity. Likewise, if there is a local community group for gay and lesbian teens—but not one yet for gender-variant, genderqueer, or transgender teens, your child may find some solace in making connection with such groups.

Be Prepared

Teenagers get into lots of unexpected situations. Some of these will be mere mishaps, but others may be more serious. Unfortunately, your trans teen runs a greater risk than the average teen of encountering problems with the police. We recommend that any transgender teenager carry on their person, at all times, a notarized letter from their doctor or therapist explaining that they are transgender. The letter should emphasize the need for sensitivity and privacy around this issue. This letter may help redirect the police officer from pressing the transgender issue as the crime or from revealing the information too broadly. We know that teens are highly unlikely to be prepared unless you help them out. Resize the letter to a wallet-size card and take it to a copy store to be laminated. Make sure the card folds over so it is discreet. Then take your teen wallet-shopping and tuck this card into a pocket where it will be hidden until needed. A sample letter is offered in Appendix 2 of this book.

In a number of situations across the country police officers have put a transgender teenager's life in danger by spreading word of the child's gender status. Although we truly hope that your teen will never have reason to produce that letter from their wallet, it is reassuring to you as a parent to know that they have it.

Finally, to further their safety, make sure that your child always has a way to reach you by supplying them with a cell phone. You should also have a conversation reassuring them that if they are ever in danger, or just suspect they might be getting into a situation they possibly can't handle, they should call you, and no matter the hour or their location, you will come and get them without judgment or questions.

Right before this book went to press, several tragedies occurred with gender-nonconforming teens as victims. We are aware that the world is still not a truly safe place for transgender, gender-nonconforming, and lesbian and gay teens. While no one can ever fully anticipate a violent reaction from others, we urge parents to have a conversation with their kids about personal safety that is as honest as possible. We sincerely hope that with continued societal education, such reactions will soon become a distant reality.

Chapter 4

Start Where You Are: Moving from Damaging to Effective Parenting Practices

THIS CHAPTER IS BASED ON findings of the Family Acceptance Project (FAP), based on research conducted by Caitlin Ryan, PhD, and her research team at the César E. Chávez Institute at San Francisco State University (SFSU). If you cite this chapter, please acknowledge the work of the Family Acceptance Project in informing our discussion. FAP has identified specific family and caregiver behaviors that promote the well-being of LGBT and gender-variant children and that, respectively, protect against or increase their risk for negative health and mental health outcomes. Specific findings of the Family Acceptance Project are marked with an asterisk (*). The project's research is forthcoming.

All parents love their children. And all parents want to do what is right for them. Sometimes it takes time to be able to do what is best for your child. That's OK—just start from where you are. We do not expect you to be perfect parents. But the small steps you take toward greater

Caitlin Ryan and the Family Acceptance Project

Caitlin Ryan is a clinical social worker and director of the Family Acceptance Project, a major community research, intervention and training initiative studying "the impact of family acceptance and rejection on the health, mental health, and well-being of lesbian, gay, bisexual and transgender youth." She recently found a few moments to talk with us about her research on gender-nonconforming and transgender young people and their families. Our questions and her responses follow:

How has the study of gender identity changed?
I think that important underlying work has been done by scholars like Anne Fausto-Sterling to begin to open up our language and understanding of gender identity and expression. Gender-variant adults, adolescents, and children have been challenging communities, schools, families, health services, and the workplace to respect their innate gender expression, which is making people rethink and reframe concepts of male and female. Having quality research is essential to help inform policies to normalize social acceptance of the full range of gender expression.

What has your research shown about transgender children?
Our research for the Family Acceptance Project has shown that specific behaviors that parents may engage in to try to help their transgender children are actually very harmful, such as trying to change their gender expression or forcing them to dress or behave or speak in ways that are not natural for them, to try to make their children fit cultural expectations of gender behavior. Instead of helping their children, these parents are teaching their

children to disrespect themselves—that there is something wrong with them, that who they are is bad and unnatural. We shouldn't be surprised that so many children who are rejected by their families engage in high-risk behaviors and use alcohol or drugs to try to cope as young people and adults.

So how can parents best support their transgender and gender-variant children?
The most important thing that parents can do to support their transgender children is to support their gender expression, not try to change, demean, or constrict their child's gender expression. And to let their children know that they love them. It's a very beautiful thing to watch these children open up and be who they are. Many parents in our study talked about how much they had grown as a result of parenting their child. In the most supportive families, parents also saw their child as a teacher who helped them grow on a human level and expand their capacity for compassion, acceptance, and love.

For more information about the Family Acceptance Project, please visit the website: http://familyproject.sfsu.edu/.

acceptance of your child will have a huge impact on their future. And you can be sure they will notice and appreciate every step you take.

Finding the courage to move through your feelings allows you to discover a renewed commitment to fully support and love your amazing child. In fact, most parents of gender-variant children and teens come to realize that what must really be overcome is their own fear and expectations, rather than something that is inherently wrong with their child.

While parents only want what's best for their child, parenting does not occur in a vacuum. We are painfully aware of society's intolerance for gender variance. Parents want to minimize hardships for their gender-variant and cross-gender children and teens as they mature, raising them to be confident and empowered adults. How can this be accomplished when there is so little information or understanding of gender variance in children?

Sometimes it is difficult to imagine that parents are so influential over the inner worlds of their children. It is an awesome responsibility. Parents' responses to their children's gender variance are far more influential than any other factor in their lives. When parents use effective parenting strategies, they can dramatically counteract the negativity their children experience elsewhere. Conversely, parents also have the ability to do the greatest damage to their children's self-esteem and well-being by using damaging parenting practices, however well-meaning they might seem.

So our message to parents is actually quite simple: Foster as much self-love and self-esteem in your child as you possibly can. You may not be able to change your child, but you can certainly affect how they feel about themselves. You can also equip them with skills to cope with the stresses they encounter. Every person who has a significant influence on your child is part of the wide net of acceptance that you must cast to create a fully realized, happy, secure child.

Damaging Parenting Practices

Research from the Family Acceptance Project shows that behaviors which children experience as rejecting significantly increase their risk for negative health and mental health problems. These rejecting behaviors undermine a child's self-esteem and feelings of self-worth. It should not be surprising that many youth who end up in the foster care system or who run away or become homeless are gender-variant and transgender.

Rejecting parenting is damaging parenting. The parental behaviors that most strongly communicate rejection are refusing to accept one's child as they are and behaving in an unkind, punitive, or unfriendly way

toward a child. Children expect, and have a right to expect, unconditional love, kindness, and support.

Supportive parenting is effective parenting. It is as simple as that. But
what are the most damaging things parents may have found themselves
doing? What are the most harmful ways parents may have been communicating rejection? Please have compassion toward yourself as you
read on. Most, if not all, parents have employed some of these practices
at one time or another. That is OK. Just do all that you can to communicate your love and support for your child now. Remember, we will all
need to start where we are.

The Myth of Defiance

We would like to clarify one misperception that causes a great deal of
confusion. Parents often perceive their gender-variant child to be acting
out, or believe their child is being rebellious by asserting their gender
variance or transgender nature. They feel, somehow, that their child's
gender variance is a form of defiance aimed at them. If a parent feels
challenged by this perceived rebelliousness, as if their authority is being
confronted, they are likely to react in a way that is punitive. In fact, this
perception of their child's behaviors actually sets their child up for
greater risks.

For example, by saying "Go change your clothes right now. You know
you can't go out of the house looking like that! Just who do you think you
are, prancing around like that?" you are indicating that you perceive your
child to be acting out. But this is not your child's intent.

When parents learn that their children are expressing an innate
part of themselves that has nothing to do with challenging parental
authority, their responses begin to change. Gender-variant and transgender children cannot help being who they are. They are not trying
to hurt you by their self-expression. Far from it: all children strive
desperately for their parents' love. With better understanding comes
empathy, and empathy permits a more measured reaction to your

child's behavior. After all, there is nothing to punish if your child has done nothing wrong. This awareness allows families to react to their children in ways that will support development of a strong sense of self.

Abuse—Physical or Verbal*

> I have been really mean to my child. We have spanked him. We won't get him the toys or clothes he begs for. We punish him when he tries to act like a girl. We send him to his room when he puts on his sister's clothes. No one has told us how to parent a child like this. I am not proud of what we have done to him. We thought it would work and he would just stop. Now we realize he can't stop. It's the way he is. Do you know how bad it feels to have punished my child for something he can't stop? But what else can I do? How can I go outside with a boy who wants to be a girl? —Parent of a 7-year-old gender-variant boy

Although it may be your inclination to try to beat or punish the gender variance out of your child—and you will not be alone if this is the approach you have taken—this is one of the most damaging things you can do to your child. Physically hurting your child in an attempt to get them to change who they are is not only completely ineffective, it puts your child at very high risk for suicide.

Hurtful statements such as "You disgust me" and "I want to throw up just being near you," or "How could I have made a child like you?" are more damaging than you can possibly imagine. Even if you are feeling these things, keep them to yourself; it will be far less damaging than speaking them. Work to temper your outward reactions so that even if you are struggling inside, it is less likely that your child will see this communicated. It may be unrealistic to expect you not to have these feelings, as it takes time to come to acceptance. Remember, start where you are—but do start.

Excluding the Child from Family Activities*

When parents are struggling with the shame they experience around their child's gender variance, a common response is to exclude the child from family events and activities to avoid being embarrassed by them. Although it may not seem blatant to you, what is communicated to the child is that they must change or they won't be a welcome member of the family.

Here are some examples of such directives. Some may be familiar to you from past struggles with your child:

"There is no way you are going to Easter dinner dressed like that. You have two choices—go put on presentable clothes right now, or stay home. And don't pull that kind of stunt with me again."

"Grandma's birthday celebration is next week. We would like you to come. But if you want to come you are going to have to pull it together so you look normal. We are not having a fairy in our family."

"You know we are about to take a photo for our Christmas card. Please go put on the outfit I bought for you and take off those crazy dress-up clothes or I'm going to finally throw them away."

Another way parents exclude their gender-variant, transgender, or gay and lesbian child is by walking a few steps ahead of them as a subconscious means of distancing themselves from them.

Your child is a part of your family and not something to be hidden away. But it is a challenge to know how to handle these situations. Perhaps a meeting in the middle is the best you can expect from yourself right now. For example, "I know we have a formal dinner coming up at Grandma's house in a few weeks. Maybe we could go shopping together to find an outfit that you feel comfortable in." Then, when you are shopping together, see how far you can push your own comfort level to meet your child's clothing preferences so that both you and your child feel that a solution has been reached.

**Blocking Access to Gender-variant or Lesbian/Gay Friends,
Activities, and Resources***

Many parents feel that if they could just keep their child away from the
influence of other kids like them, their child might go back to "normal." This is the age-old "hanging out with the wrong crowd" argument. The unfortunate thing is that by removing or forbidding contact
with other people whom your child can relate to, you are only isolat-
ing them further. Children may then just turn inward, as there is no
place left for them to freely express themselves or even see a future for
themselves. Blocking access to like-minded community and friends
can greatly increase the risks your child faces.

Do the following comments sound familiar?

"If you just spend your time focused on your schoolwork and not
those freak friends of yours, you'd find this whole transgender thing
would just go away. You are just doing it to be part of the group."

"You are not allowed to see, talk to, or be on the Internet with anyone from that gay group at your school. If I catch you doing that I am
sending you to military school. And they don't take too well to boys
like you there."

"When you are out of the house you can spend time with those
kinds of people. While you live here I will not allow it."

By stigmatizing other people like your child, or not allowing your
child to attend events to learn more about people like them, you are
communicating your lack of respect for who your child is. To the child,
it can feel as if you are trying to trap them in your reality, a reality that
does not allow any room for them. For a transgender or gender-
variant child or teen this can feel as if you are taking away their air,
their very lifeline to the future. If you cannot believe in a possible
future for them that is positive, and they cannot connect to one themselves by interacting with role models, it can be hard for them to hold
on to a will to live.

Blaming Your Child for the Discrimination They Face*

One of the most damaging parenting practices you can employ is to blame your child for the discrimination they face. Comments like the following may be based in frustration and concern for their safety, but they will not feel loving from your child's perspective:

"Don't come running to me if you get beat up. You are just asking for it. Just be sure to take it like a man when they come to see if you are really a man or a woman."

"But honey, you know you wouldn't be teased like that if you didn't walk that way."

"What the hell did you expect, going out of the house dressed like that?"

Your child hears that there is something wrong with who they are and that it is their fault. They hear that they are to blame and deserve to be treated with disrespect. Some people can better understand the injustice of this when they realize how similar it is to blaming a woman for being raped. Your child is not "acting out," or "asking for it," but simply engaging in natural self-expression. Would you tell a child of color to simply paint their skin white so they could avoid discrimination? Absolutely not—you would actively teach your child resiliency skills, and work to build their self-esteem. The same is true for your gender-variant or transgender child. Although "passing" as a typically gendered person might make everyone more comfortable, it is asking your child to play-act in order to be accepted. It is asking them to succumb to peer pressure and to follow mainstream notions in order to participate in daily life.

Parental Denigration and Ridicule*

He is so lonely. His brothers are embarrassed by him. We are embarrassed by him. Why won't he just change? Why can't he be normal? I want to accept him. Nobody told me that is what I should

do. I feel so bad. We have been very mean to him. We didn't under-
stand. But how do we accept him? It's embarrassing. What will my
family say? He asks every day why God made him this way. I do
too. I did not know I was making things harder for him. —Parent
of a 6-year-old gender-variant boy

When you speak to your child in disrespectful ways—whether with
words or with body language—you communicate your rejection and
lack of acceptance. This behavior includes rolling your eyes, imitating
how they walk, making fun of the clothes they wear or how they talk,
and imitating how they hold their body. It also includes leaving the
room when they enter it, or moving away from them at the table. Parents often target their gender-variant and transgender children with their
ridicule because they are so afraid for their children and afraid that their
child's variance reflects poorly on them.

Having a child who has special needs does not give a parent or anyone else liberty to ridicule them. A child who is gender-variant or transgender today has special needs. They are not disabled, or mentally ill, or
medically ill—but their needs are different from the average child's. They
deserve the same love, kindness, and respect as any child.

Religion-Based Condemnation

I told him God would never make him be a girl in a boy's body.
God doesn't make mistakes, only people make mistakes. So he
was obviously mistaken and needed to repent. —Parent of an
8-year-old gender-variant boy

Supportive families use their religious values and beliefs to support
their child's diversity. But telling children that God will punish them
because of their sexual orientation or gender expression increases their
risk for health and mental health problems. Telling your child to pray
in order to change who they are is using religion to condemn them.

Because religion is an important part of family life, religious condemnation takes away an important source of solace and support for children of religious backgrounds.

Many parents find that at a certain point their transgender child rejects and resists religion, often refusing outright to go to church. Parents who feel that their child's gender is at odds with God often believe their child's rejection of religion is further proof that something is wrong with their child. However, it is really not surprising that numerous transgender teens and young adults become disillusioned with God after praying so persistently to God to let them become a girl or a boy and receiving no answer. Once these young people are allowed the freedom to more fully express themselves as transgender, they frequently return to their religion, or find a different religious or spiritual practice that better suits their new lives.

Distress, Denial, and Shame*

He used to say very often, "I am a girl," inside and outside the home. We told him every time, we are happy that you are a boy. It started getting very repetitive and annoying to the point where we offered him prizes if he went a week without saying it. That made him stop. After watching the show on 20/20 with Barbara Walters, I asked him what he felt like inside himself, if he felt like a boy or a girl, and his answer was that he felt like a girl. Then I asked him if he wanted to be a girl, and his answer made me cry when he said, I don't know, Mommy, what do you want me to be?
—Parent of a 6-year-old gender-variant boy

When you communicate to your child that you are ashamed of them, it cuts to the quick. Although many parents come right out and tell their child how ashamed they are, others communicate it just as loudly through indirect statements and actions. For example, the Family Acceptance Project found that many families with gender-variant children displayed only photographs of them taken when they were younger and the parents had more influence on their gender presentation. When their child stopped being gender-conforming, the parents no longer displayed photos that documented their activities and inclusion in the family. This was in marked contrast to their other adolescent children or relatives, whose photographs were prominently displayed showing them as youths or young adults.

When your child sees that they are causing you great distress and shame, they internalize this pressure. No one wants to be a burden. It is just as damaging to communicate denial of your child's gender variance or transgender identity. This denial can take various forms—for example, if your son insists that he is really a girl, saying to him, "No, you are a boy. Boys have penises. You have a penis. You are a boy." Or saying to a friend, "Oh, Janet thinks she's a boy. Isn't that funny?" Or simply rejecting your child by denying them the opportunity to spend time with you: " I can't go to the movies with you if you are dressed like that. You go ahead, I'll just stay home."

Silence and Secrecy*

When you require silence and secrecy around your child's gender identity or sexual orientation, you are damaging your child by teaching them to split off a core part of their identity. It makes them feel there is something inherently wrong with them if they are not allowed to talk about who they are. Likewise, it is a heavy burden to feel they must hide who they are from immediate family members, or worse yet, keep it entirely to themselves. Parents may feel they are sparing other family members from something they can't handle, but your child is not a burden to be overcome. Some parents may covertly ask for secrecy while appearing to be accepting. For example:

"It is fine if you are transgender. Just don't tell anyone. When you leave for college you can live that way, but for now we'll just keep this our little secret."

"I don't think your dad could handle this. So how about we just don't tell him. Actually, I don't think you should tell anyone. We live in such a conservative town, you never know what could happen to you if people found out."

In these statements your child hears that their very reality will never be accepted, so the only way to survive within the family is to live a lie and to hide their core identity.

Pressure to Enforce Gender Conformity*

Indeed, even the most well-meaning parents pressure their kids to conform to gender presentation expectations. They may do this to help their kids become more socially acceptable, or to protect their kids from harm, or to make themselves more comfortable. But the communication is always the same—there is something wrong with the child's natural way of expressing themselves:

"Come on, you can't go to the barbeque dressed like that. You'll be the laughingstock of the party. Can't you just tone it down?"

"I think it would be best if you just wore those kinds of things at home."

"I think it's time to practice walking. You just plow through a room. You need to be more graceful."

Damaging parenting can be both obvious and subtle. It is not always blatant, like physical abuse. Every parent has probably engaged in damaging parenting practices at some time. To improve your parenting skills, try to develop as many positive or neutral techniques as possible. In two-parent families, if one parent is rejecting and the other is supportive, the positive and supportive parent may not always be able to counteract the impact of the rejecting parent.

If there is disagreement within the household or between households about how to approach your child's gender, the most important thing you can agree on is to reduce the rejection your child experiences, overtly and subtly, at home. If you can agree to minimize the behaviors outlined in this section and to strive for at least neutral parenting responses, your child will be significantly better off. Your parenting has far-reaching effects—it touches your children not only at this time of their lives, but in their adult lives as well. You have the power to make a huge difference in their lives. You must wield that power with great care.

Effective Parenting Practices

Supportive Family Environment*

The parenting practices that follow apply to gender-variant children, lesbian, gay, and bisexual children, and transgender children. These are parenting practices that we encourage you to follow. They are based on the solid body of research conducted by the Family Accept-ance Project. The parenting practices described below have a direct and significant impact on rates of suicide, drug use, HIV-related risk, depression, outlook on life, and homelessness—in other words, on a child's current and future mental and physical health. As you might imagine, the happiest and most well adjusted children are the ones who know they are loved and supported. If parents help their children create a solid foundation for their identity, they help their children to be happy, healthy—and alive.

The single most important factor in promoting lifelong health and well-being for your child is creating a supportive home environment. Family is the center of a child's and a teenager's life. And parental acceptance is the number one determining factor for long-term out-comes for gender-variant and cross-gender children and teens. Pro-viding a safe and supportive home environment gives them a buffer from the hardships they may face outside the home and reinforces a strong sense of self for them as someone lovable and good. If this doesn't come so easily for you, find support from an empathetic, knowledgeable family therapist, and work on following the sugges-tions in this chapter.

Parents Can Change the World

Parents have an amazing ability to positively influence their own children and the children they come in contact with. Parents are agents of change. You can embrace this role actively, knowing that the way you present gender to young children will influence them for the rest of their lives. By encouraging gender equity and gender diversity you allow no room for discrimination and bias. Just as you would stand up against other inequities and stereotypes, make it a point to do so for gender inequity and gender stereotypes. In so doing, you support all children. By celebrating all people in their right to natural expression you are also boosting the confidence and self-esteem of gender-variant children.

> *We went to see a therapist to talk about our son's issue. I was more interested in getting information for us as parents, and in learning tools for how to better deal with this. In this first session was when we faced the reality, when we heard the words, "this sounds like a child who may be transgender."* —Parent of a 7-year-old gender-variant boy

The sanctity of your home as a place of safety and support is paramount. This means a home without ridicule, shame, punishment, or rejection—a home where every member is valued and accepted and loved for who they are. This is the most significant thing you can provide for your child. Everything else builds upon this.

When Parenting Approaches Differ

It is not uncommon for parents to react differently to their child's gender variance. Typically one parent feels more comfortable allowing their child's self-expression, while the other feels that they are thereby "encouraging" it. As much as possible, strive for a unified approach. We understand that this is not always possible.

It's been hard to see that our son doesn't behave like other boys his own age. It's been a lot harder for me than my husband. He is always the one pulling me back down to earth. All in all, my husband has been cooler about this. I have been uneasy but we have not had any big conflicts over this. We both agree that we want our son to be happy. —Parent of a 7-year-old gender-variant boy

Some parents differ primarily over what behaviors are allowed outside the home and what should remain within the home. This is an important issue to work out. Although it is tricky, you can still create a

When Parents are Divorced or Separated

In cases of divorce or separation, things can get contentious if one parent challenges the other's parenting approaches in regard to their child's gender variance. Do whatever you can to reach amicable agreements by availing yourself of family therapy. At the present it is in your family's best interest to keep this issue out of Family Court Services. It may mean agreeing to different rules at different homes. Although this may not be the ideal solution for your child, it is far better than a court mandate restricting your child's gender expression. As times change and general understanding of transgender issues increases, the court system may serve your family, but that is not the case now.

My child's father is the biggest issue. For my child's fourth birthday my sister gave him a doll and he was so excited, but when his dad saw it he started yelling. I knew at that point that my child had to basically lead a dual life, and not show his dad his girl side. —Divorced parent of a 7-year-old gender-variant boy supportive home environment. This can be an increased challenge if your child has more than one home. But coming to agreement about freedom and respect within the home goes a very long way as you navigate together how to approach the outside world.

However, if there is division within your home or between homes and you cannot reach an agreement with another parent about the limits of expression, make sure that your child knows that *you* are fully supportive of who they are. In this way, though your child may experience pressure or rejection from one or more parents, your child recognizes you as their ally. If there is division within your home, it is all the more important to read on about the other significant ways parents can influence the current and future well-being of their children. Just know that you will need to employ these techniques both outside and within your own home.

Of course, the goal is for children to experience full acceptance within their own homes. But, as we have discussed, true acceptance can take years. If you decide to maintain your existing family unit through the period of coming to terms—despite significant discrepancies in your parenting approaches to your gender-variant child—you may need to establish some hard and fast household rules to ensure the emotional safety and well-being of your child. Do everything you can to reduce your child's exposure to damaging parenting practices, improving their health and safety. Do everything you can to counteract or minimize your child's perception that they are the cause of the household stress and conflict. Each family will navigate this tricky territory differently.

Components of Powerful Parenting

In the rest of this chapter we outline the very specific qualities that research has shown are the most influential ways of demonstrating support to gender-nonconforming children. These are the primary components of powerful parenting for all children. No parent is perfect, but it can be incredibly reassuring to know that there is a road map you can follow for directly improving the quality of life for your children.

Some of the following will come easily to you; some may require quite a bit of stretch and growth to achieve. Just know that every step you take toward demonstrating your acceptance and support of your child is significant.

Keep a Log or Journal

Having guided many families through this journey of acceptance, Stephanie can tell you that it is very valuable to keep a log or a journal. You can look back every six months and see how far you have come in your journey toward understanding and acceptance. You can also note the progress of your partner or other important family members or friends. Of course, you can also use your journal as a self-reflective tool along the way, or simply as a practical place to notate both your own journey and the markers of your child.

It is beautiful to review these logs. You can see how your struggle and agony gradually turned into acceptance and ease. You can also see all the hard work and the many steps that it took for everyone to get here.

Require Respect within the Family*

Within your immediate and extended family it is essential that you tolerate only kindness and respect toward your gender-variant or cross-gender child. You may not be able to change anyone's opinions or views about your parenting or your child, but you can dictate what you and your child are exposed to.

It is important to make clear that each person in the family deserves equal respect. If you have differing opinions, that is your prerogative, but negative feelings need to be contained and not communicated through words, snorts, facial expressions, or other forms of body language.

Although it can be scary to explicitly request respect from extended family members, it is not an unreasonable request. In fact, many parents report a great sense of relief after insisting on basic kindness from relatives:

> We told my parents that if they could not refrain from negative talk about our child in our presence, then we would no longer be able to spend time with them. We clarified that we meant that there would be NO negative talk about our son to him, us, or any of his siblings. And, there would be no negative talk about him to others in our presence. This took guts, but we had no choice. Well, actually we did have a choice, and we were making it. We chose our son over others. That's what parents must do. —Parents of a gender-variant 8-year-old boy

> I come from Mexico. I have a very big family. They do not respect people who are gay, and have a lot of prejudice against things they think are gay. I had to tell them, my son may be like that, and my son does those things. I love my son. I love him so much. I will do anything for him. I will not stop loving him because he likes his hair long. I will not stop loving him because he likes to dance. But if they cannot love him for who he is, then we cannot be with them. Some of my family has stayed with us. They love our little guy. Others, well, we don't see them anymore. —Parent of a gender-fluid 7-year-old

> I told my family we would not be coming to Thanksgiving this year. I explained that the way they treat our gender-variant daughter is hurting her so much that she cries about it between visits. We decided that her happiness and self-esteem are more valuable to us than our family. I acknowledged that it made all of us sad, but for us, it was the right decision. We love our daughter and stand by who she is. My mom was stunned into silence. I thought she was disapproving of me. But when I went to say

- Toys are just toys.
- Colors are just colors.
- Clothes are just clothes.
- Families come in all shapes and sizes.
- Different people like different things.
- Respect means keeping our minds open.
- Having open minds means giving people freedom to be who they want to be.

good-bye, she was crying. She said she was ashamed about her behavior and she would talk to the rest of the family about this. We haven't heard back from them yet. I guess we have drawn our line in the sand. The next move is theirs. —Parent of a gender-variant 10-year-old

Express Love and Support for Your Child's Gender Expression*

Follow your child's lead. Don't foster, don't deny. This is their experience, we're just the helpers. —Parent of a 20-year-old transwoman

As we have stated, current research from the Family Acceptance Project shows that supporting your child's gender expression is one of the most important things you can do to promote your child's well-being. That is easy to say, but what does it mean exactly to express love and support for your child's gender expression?

Supporting your child's gender expression means allowing them to choose, without pressure, what clothes they wear, how they play, what they play with, what toys they are allowed to have, what accessories they have, and how they decorate their room. Fully supporting your child's gender expression also includes allowing them to wear their hair in ways that are preferable to them. However, families have different levels of comfort with gender-variant expression inside and outside the home, so for some, the freedom of expression does not extend to hairstyles.

If you took gender programming out of the picture, clothes would simply be clothes, toys would simply be toys, and colors would simply be colors. There would be no concept of assigning a gender to certain clothes, or toys, or colors. When you think about it, it is rather odd to consider objects as inherently gendered.

It is helpful to question what exactly is threatened if your child has preferences for things that are considered to be for the "other" gender. It was not too long ago that a girl in pants was a radical idea, or a female athlete was a radical idea. But it is still a radical idea for most to imagine a boy with a collection of dolls, or a boy in a twirly skirt.

> *He used to say that he wished he were a girl. When we asked him why, his reason was that he liked long hair, to which we would reply that he didn't have to be a girl to have long hair. Since he was about 3 years old he's been expressing [his gender variance] in words, and before that he would play with towels, baby blankets, scarves, tablecloths, wrapping them all around his waist and pretending they were skirts. We spent one Christmas with my family and my mom was very concerned, she talked to me and my husband and told us we were being too permissive with our son and he could get sexually confused.* —Parent of a 7-year-old gender-variant boy

There is still a tremendous amount of sexism interwoven with gender expression. Before you can fully love and support your child you need to become aware of your own sexism and learn to work actively against it. There is a fear that males who express stereotypically female preferences are not true males—that their masculinity, and their assumed heterosexuality, are somehow threatened by a preference in colors, fabrics, toys, or hairstyles. In fact, if we were all given the freedom to express ourselves without enforcement of gender conformity, personal creativity would extend far and wide. There would be less conformity, less repression, and greater freedom of thought.

Clothes

Clothes are a huge means of communicating gender. Instead of being segregated by styles, colors, or fabrics, clothing departments are segregated by gender. We know what clothing we are expected to wear to fit smoothly into the social order. As a result, your child's simply preferring clothes from the other department can seem like an act of transgression. For many children, clothing is a statement of personal preference, not always a statement about gender or gender identity. However, it is important to allow transgender children to choose clothes that clearly reflect their gender to others. We recommend that you allow your children to dress themselves in the ways that feel most comfortable to them within your current comfort zone. Try not to restrict what they wear based on perception of gender. Shop in both departments and try to create a wardrobe you both can live with.

> It was so difficult to get our (trans) son dressed. He would spend forever in front of the mirror adjusting the front of his pants, and his socks. He could show us where pockets were on boy's pants vs. girl's pants. He could show us how the socks were different. To him clothes and posture were like a gender uniform. He could show us how you hold your body when you are a boy or when you are a girl. Now, mind you, this gender observer was 3 years old! —Parent of an 8-year-old transboy

> We finally compromised; our gender-variant son could wear whatever he wanted out of the house as long as it wasn't a dress. Dresses are reserved for wearing at home. But he can shop anywhere in the store for any clothes that he wants. He has lots of pink, ruffles, and flares, and flower prints, orange, and purple clothes. Lots of appliqué. He just likes beautiful clothes. If we could sew rainbow

ribbons and sparkles onto everything he owned he would be in heaven. He has never said he wasn't a boy. But he loves these clothes. He plays with boys and girls. He loves to play rough-and-tumble and dress-up. His behaviors seem really balanced. His gender identity is solidly male. But his presentation is fluid. Or at least that's how we see it. Others think he dresses like a girl. —Parent of a 6-year-old gender-variant boy

Many parents report that they really didn't understand the extent to which their child was gender-variant or the reality that they were truly cross-gender until it was time to attend an event where formal clothes were mandatory. Here is where gender-variant girls refuse to wear dresses, and boys are heartbroken at having to wear a suit, or at not being allowed to wear a dress. The dread, stress, and agony the whole family endures trying to get the child to wear the unwanted clothes brings big issues to the surface—for example, whom are you trying to please by forcing your child to conform, and are you damaging your child in the process? Our recommendation, once again, it to push yourself to the edge of your comfort zone and see if you can agree on an outfit that allows your child to express themselves while allowing you to feel comfortable, as well. This gets easier with time.

We had to attend a wedding. My daughter needed to wear a dress, there was no way around it. She always wore pants or shorts, but this was a wedding. She kicked, and screamed, hid under the bed, threatened to run away. She was hysterical. She insisted that she would only wear the same clothes as her brother. This was the day of the wedding. She would not calm down. We were all yelling at her and each other. Still there was no answer, and we couldn't drag her to the wedding. We ended up leaving her at home at the last minute with a neighbor. We were furious at her for ruining the day for us. Then at age 13 she told us she was transgender. Looking back, the first thing we pointed to in our minds as a marker of this

*was that wedding. We should have known then. But who would
ever think that their daughter was transgender?* —Parent of a
15-year-old transboy

Behaviors

Supporting your child's gender means refraining from negative comments about the toys your child likes to play with, how they act, what
they enjoy, and how they express themselves. Not surprisingly, a supportive response actually enhances your child's self-esteem.

For example, if your gender-variant young son says, "Look, Daddy!
I made this castle and I am the princess. Let me show you the princess
dance of the fairies," you could respond in several ways. You could be
negative: "Take that outfit off! I don't want to see you prancing around
like a girl." Or more neutral: "Not right now, honey, why don't you show
your mother?" Or supportive: "Let me see! That is a really neat castle you
built. I can see it took you lots of time. I am ready to see the dance—is
this a good place to sit?" It may be difficult for you to get to the point of
acceptance, but how your child will shine when you do.

Support for your child's gender-variant behaviors means finding ways
for your child to express themselves that feel best for them. This may
involve making sure they have access to activities they enjoy or friends
with similar interests. And it may mean that you end up spending time
doing activities or being with children you never could have imagined.

Toys

Toys, like clothing, have become heavily gendered. Many toy stores are
divided according to gender, just like clothing departments. It can be
alarming for any parent (not just the parent of a transgender child) to
see the strict division of toys in larger toy stores or department stores.
Entire aisles are devoted to boys' toys—building blocks, robots, action
figures, superheroes—constructed in shades of brown, black, gray, blue,
red, and green. One aisle over, it's the girls' area, and everything is pink

or pastel—princess outfits, tea party sets, dolls, Barbies™, ponies, and other cute little animals. There seems to be very little middle ground in toy selection once children leave their toddler years.

Nonetheless, what a child likes to play with and how they like to play with it is an individual part of self-expression. After all, like colors, no toy is only a boy's or a girl's toy—it is just a toy. Providing each child with a full range of toys to play with allows for full exploration of various parts of self. Give your child toys of various textures, colors, and styles, toys for imaginative play, and toys for mental or educational play.

It can be a challenge for parents to remember not to preselect toys for their child based on their gender. Most parents limit the toys their children can play with, and try to redirect children who cross the gender line. Children also monitor toy use among their peers by telling a friend that a certain toy is "a girl's toy" or "a boy's toy" with scorn in their voice.

By shopping in independent toy stores instead of the big chains, you hold a chance of being able to let your child select a full range of toys not based on gender. Play sets based on imagination let all children build a world they can inhabit and rule. Some online toy sites offer wooden doll houses, gnome houses, knight dolls, pirate ships, fairies, and even "feng-shui" dolls, all well constructed and appealing to a wide range of children. This variety may also ease the pressure on family members when shopping for your child.

Accessories/Toothbrushes/Belongings

Allow your child to select the decorations for their room, their backpacks, sleeping bags, toothbrushes, and the like. It can be a small but liberating way to give your child some sense of personal gender expression. Avoid steering your child toward the commercialization of gender. Let your child pick freely, or if that is too worrisome to you, go out of your way to find gender-neutral choices. If you would rather your daughter not have a male superhero on her sleeping bag, or your son a princess toothbrush, it may be best to let your child choose from items that are simply colorful or patterned rather than inherently gendered or character-based.

If your teenager chooses to wear accessories typically chosen by the other sex, the best response is to compliment their choices. The next best response is not to comment at all—have a neutral response. After all, by the time they are this age they are aware that they are going against the gender grain, and they want to do it anyway. Even though you might want to change them, you won't be able to, so rather than provide a disparaging response, it's better to say nothing at all.

Inside the House / Outside the House

Each family has their own boundaries about what is acceptable for their child. In some families parents try to contain the gender-variant behaviors of their children. This may be so that others are not made uncomfortable and also to prevent the possibility of their child being ridiculed. But by doing so, they are communicating to their child that social pressure should be accommodated at all cost. This form of parenting can potentially communicate shame to your child. Once again, it may be valuable for you to examine whom you are trying to protect by encouraging your child to remain undisclosed out in the world.

> For Christmas my son just wanted a dress, that was all he was asking for. He got a fairy skirt, and that was the only present he paid attention to. He wanted at the beginning to wear it outside the house, but I said no, as I felt others would laugh at him, and he accepted that. —Parent of a 6-year-old gender-variant boy

Often, families start out with tight boundaries about what they will and will not permit outside the home. Such limits work well when the child is only moderately gender-variant, and can learn to understand and navigate where and when it is considered appropriate to wear certain clothes. However, for significantly gender-variant or transgender children, asking them to limit their self-expression because of social pressure can cause great stress. Over time, if parents see that their child is emotionally shutting down in order to leave the house looking as the parents wish, it is a good idea to loosen up on the rules. There will come a time when your child is old enough to refuse your control.

Parents who have gender-variant boys often begin by allowing their son to have girls' toys, decorations, and clothes at home. Other families set limits about where their son can wear dresses, or where their daughter can go in a suit and a tie, or how short she can wear her hair.

> We have tried to explain to him that there is a differentiation between home and the outside world in relevance to what is accepted by others. He used to like to bring his Barbie™ doll with him when we were going out, but if he saw boys approaching he would quickly hand it over to me to put in my purse. Inside the house, he loves to dress up as a girl and wishes he were one.
> —Parent of a 6-year-old gender-variant boy

Over time, many families that have different rules for inside and outside the home realize that while they are providing their child with a very important outlet for self-expression, they are also communicating to their child that their child is embarrassing to them. Not only to prevent this feeling of shame in their child but also to allow their child the freedom of personal expression, more and more families of strongly gender-variant children are taking the brave leap and allowing their children to be themselves wherever they go.

> My son expresses himself as he is—a normal little boy. When he was in kindergarten he was very depressed and withdrawn. He never played with other kids. Despite some bad advice from a "great child psychiatrist" who told us only to let him dress like a boy at home, we started letting him dress like a boy [everywhere]. This changed his life. When we saw that change, we knew he was really a boy. —Parent of a 7-year-old transboy

However, we strongly encourage you to insist that your child's school receive gender diversity training if your boy plans to start wearing dresses or other "feminine" attire to school. That way, the school will have greater understanding of how to support your child and how to respond effectively to questions from both parents and students and to potential harassment and bullying. This proactive approach will help keep your child physically and emotionally safe when outside the home.

Bathrooms

Many transgender and gender-variant children and teens have great anxiety over the use of public bathrooms. If you have not experienced aggression and rejection in the bathroom, you may find it difficult to imagine what this feels like.

For transgender children and teens, the bathroom can be a scary place that symbolizes their differentness. If your child is living in accordance with their gender identity, they may be especially afraid they will be found out in the bathroom. If they identify as transgender and are not yet living in accordance with their gender identity, they can feel like an imposter in the bathroom. If they are gender-variant and present differently from the gender of the bathroom they enter, they may be questioned or subjected to abuse. This can be scary, especially for a child or teen who identifies as male but presents in a female way in the male restroom.

The issues are complex. Everyone should be entitled to a safe place to go to the bathroom, but it isn't that easy. You need to teach your child how to navigate bathroom safety. In Chapter 7, The Educational System and Your Family, we cover how to do this in educational facilities; in this section we discuss the use of bathrooms outside of school.

When your child is young, the easiest solution is to take them into the bathroom with you. However, by age 8 or 9, this may cease to be a viable option. Fortunately, by that age, you can usually have some frank conversations about the situation with them. The key is to balance what you say with knowing that you do not want your child to develop a fear or phobia of restrooms.

> *Our trans son has a huge fear of bathrooms. This came from his stepmom. She kept scaring him about going into the men's bathrooms when he was young. Now he won't go into them on his own. He passes fully as male—but he will risk not going rather than go into a men's room. Everywhere we go he looks for single-stall bathrooms that do not say male or female. This can actually be a very big deal if we are out without his dad to escort him into the men's room.* —Parent of a 10-year-old transboy

Older children need a realistic discussion about what they might encounter in the bathrooms they enter. From there you can start to brainstorm options. For example, teach older children to use single-stall, gender-neutral bathrooms or family bathrooms when available. Help them to scout out such bathrooms in places along their regular routes. Some restaurants and cafés allow people to use their bathrooms, which are often private, safe, single stalls. Airports, libraries, and malls also often have family restrooms that are single stalls.

In certain circumstances it may be best to tell your child to use the bathroom that aligns with their presentation, rather than their identity. Talk with your child about this and help them learn when to make this choice. This is important—your child's safety is paramount. It is up to you to help your child navigate the best ways to do this.

> *We had to explain to our 14-year-old son that he will not be safe if he wears skirts into a public men's bathroom. He didn't believe us. It is fine at his school. But his school is not the "real" world. He attends a very small, liberal school. We had to get much more graphic than we had intended, because we truly felt he was risking his life by going into who knows what bathroom at what hour dressed like that. He says we are cramping his style. We know we*

are trying to keep him safe. Yes, we let him dress like that, but we can't send him to the wolves unaware. We finally came to an agreement about public bathroom use. —Parent of a 14-year-old genderqueer son

Zero Tolerance for Disrespect, Negative Comments, or Pressure

Learning terminology and understanding concepts of gender variance is critical. Finding positive, supportive ways to communicate gender variance and using affirmative language communicates your support to your child and to everyone else. Without positive language, you may really struggle when you try to discuss this with others. Learning to speak up in support of your child can take time, but it helps ensure that your child has a safe environment in which to live, play, and learn.

A concrete way to demonstrate ongoing support and acceptance of your gender-variant child is to tolerate no negative comments about your child, from anyone. Follow this practice whether or not your child is with you at the time the comment is made. After standing up for your child, you may find you prefer to leave the discussion. Or, you may find you can make your point more powerfully if you stay. We recommend that you proceed in whatever way you are most comfortable with, as long as you support your child.

If you become aware of negative comments or actions directed toward your child when you are not present, you will be most supportive by directly discussing the issue with the appropriate person. For example, you may find out that your child was bullied at school. It is essential to report it and to emphasize that this is not acceptable. Similarly, if you experience a negative reaction to your child while you are together— someone on the street rolls their eyes and imitates your child's walk, say—rather than ignoring it, it is more supportive of your child to address it. Of course, try to do so in a way that communicates firmness and respect. You might say, "I'm sorry you feel the need to tease people. It is not a becoming quality."

Sticking up for your child in your home, in your community, and out in the greater world is one of the most effective ways of demonstrating support for gender-variant children. Aside from improving their health and well-being, it also models justice and a strong sense of values. When your child knows that you will stand up for them, their self-worth increases exponentially.

Engage in Open and Supportive Communication*

One of the most crucial tools you have for keeping your children healthy and helping them become well-adjusted is to walk with them on their journey of self-discovery and self-expression. To do so, you must stay in frequent communication with them.

Gender identity and gender expression unfold over time. It is important to witness and support the natural gender identity development process in your child. Try not to rush it. A child with a gender-fluid expression can be very challenging and frustrating for parents. The lack of consistency in their child's gender expression can leave parents wondering just who their child really is. Some parents feel desperate to find a solid answer—male or female. This "back and forth" expression can feel crazy-making to a mind trained to see gender as static. But just be in the present with your child. Allow them to show themselves to you. Just as you do not yet know what profession they will choose when they grow up, you do not know what their gender identity or expression will be. Keep in mind that it may always remain fluid.

My son has always identified with girls and often likes to dress in girls' clothes in private, but is quite clear that he is a boy and does not want to be identified as a girl. I don't see him as transgender at this time, and I hold myself open to wherever he lands on the spectrums of gender identity and sexual orientation in the future. He told me long ago that he just wanted to be himself, which has guided me since in my parenting of him. —Parent of a 7-year-old gender-variant boy

Stay open to your child. Let them know that you are there for them. Let them know that who they are today, tomorrow, and the next day is fine with you. Tell them you look forward to knowing them as they know themselves better and better.

Because of the fluidity many children have toward gender, it may be best to refrain from using any labels with your child. If your child chooses a label, ask them about their choice and how it feels for them. Neither adults nor children enjoy being labeled by others. It feels uncomfortable and confining.

> *We had been referring to our child as transgender. Finally one day we asked him about it. He said he didn't actually think of himself as transgender. Rather, everyone else did. He thought of himself as having been a boy all of his life. He says he will use the term trans because he knows it is what people say, but he doesn't think it fits his experience. After that we tried not to use the word so much.* —Parent of a 9-year-old boy

It is best to have an air of inquisitiveness toward your child. Ask how they see themselves, what they think about, what their concerns are regarding others. What kinds of pressures do they feel, and how does that affect them? What are their deepest dreams, hopes, and fears? Questions like these let them know that you are there for them. Open-ended communication leaves room for your child's gender to evolve over time. Allow your child to be whoever they experience themselves to be.

> *One of the things I always tell people is that although we thought we had a son, we found out we have a daughter. However, our daughter may show us that she wants to be our son again, or that she feels best being both genders or neither gender, or something we don't have the words for yet. We are open. We are certainly not*

attached to her being a transgender person. We are attached to her being herself. We hope for her to always feel loved and supported by us. —Parent of a 13-year-old transgirl

Staying connected to your child and always interested in their experience will help you grow and evolve together. It will help you understand how your child frames their experience, and it will help you provide guidance and support. If your child struggles too intensely with their sense of self-worth or with gender confusion, staying connected will help you know whether your child needs additional outside support or intervention.

A Vow of Parental Acceptance*

I start here, and from wherever I am, and from this day forward, I will:

- Speak positively about my child to them and to others about them
- Take an active stand against discrimination
- Make positive comments about gender diversity
- Work with schools and other institutions to make these places safer for gender-variant, transgender, and all children
- Find gender-variant friends and create our own community
- Express admiration for my child's identity and expression, whatever direction that may take
- Volunteer for gender organizations to learn more and to further the understanding of others
- Believe my child can have a happy future

Express Concern without Expressing Rejection

Given all this information, many parents wonder how they can express natural parental concern for the well-being of their child without appearing rejecting. We want to reassure you that you can still set boundaries and express concerns; that is part of your job as a parent. Rather, it is how you express those concerns that may need to change.

For example, if your son in high school tells you that he feels he is transgender and that he plans to wear a dress to the formal dance, you have a few choices for how to respond. To yourself you may say, *No, you will not, Son.* But before you speak, take some time. What exactly are your concerns? Try to enumerate them. Part of you may feel embarrassed, part of you afraid for his safety, or afraid he is moving too fast, or you may feel he is too young to understand whether he is transgender and the implications of pushing the social envelope in this way. Then decide which parts to speak to your child about. "I imagine you have given this a lot of thought, and I am interested to hear those thoughts. I know that I am not a teenager now, it has been some time since I was in school, so my worries may not be relevant, but I'd like to speak to you about your choice to wear a dress. Do any boys wear dresses to dances at your school? How do you think others might respond? Does anyone know that this is your plan? How do they feel?"

This conversation should be gentle—not a barrage of questions, but a coming together to talk things through in a nonconfrontational manner. Your child may completely surprise you by already having considered these concerns and more.

Using the school dance again as an example, perhaps you have a transgender son who is not out yet at school but has decided the time is right and is planning to attend the dance wearing a suit. He says three friends who are fully supportive are attending the dance with him, and they have decided that the risk of physical harm is low. Perhaps the school's gay–straight alliance has given a presentation encouraging students to wear clothes that truly express themselves. You may still be left with fears for your child's safety when he leaves the dance that night, and how will he be treated at school the next day. He may look you in the eye and ask you not to worry, tell you that this is his journey. Nonetheless, discuss ways to keep him safe and whom to talk to at school if he experiences harassment. Tell him that if he ever gets into trouble because of his gender expression you will come and get him, no matter what—no questions asked. Tell him that you care about him, worry for him, support him. If you feel any embarrassment for him, or for yourself, deal with it on your own. He does not need to hear about it. The two of you should come away satisfied that your son feels supported and that you set some practical safety rules.

We are aware that the world is not as safe as we all hope it could be for transgender, gender-variant, and gender-nonconforming teens. Violence can and does happen. Not too long before this book went to press, there were several tragic events in the news, including the murder of a gender-nonconforming teenager by a classmate. We do not take the potential for violence lightly, and we hope you and your family will find the right balance between allowing your teenager to grow and express themselves and doing what you can to keep them safe. We are hopeful that as times continue to change, and understanding of transgender and gender-variant people grows, incidents of violence will become a thing of the past. Whether or not your child is openly gender-nonconforming at school, request that the school conduct gender sensitivity training to reduce gender discrimination for all.

Small Steps

These are some guidelines to follow to show your support for your gender-variant and transgender children throughout their lives. Of course, each parent and each child is unique. Give yourself credit for where you are today, reading this book, looking for answers and guidance. Every step that you take toward communicating acceptance, love, and support to your child is incredibly significant. You may not be ready to take some of the steps outlined in this chapter, yet. That's OK. Every step you take will bring you closer to your child. Get the support that you need to grow in the areas that are holding you back. After all, a parent's journey of love and acceptance for their child never really ends.

RESOURCES

Organizations
Gender Spectrum Education and Training
   http://www.genderspectrum.org/

Family Acceptance Project
   http://familyproject.sfsu.edu/

Gender Spectrum Family
   http://www.genderspectrum.org/
   Click on "Family Conference" for more information.
   National conference for families with gender-variant, gender-fluid, and transgender children.

www.mermaids.freeuk.com/
   British site for transgender kids and their families.

http://pflag.org/TNET.tnet.0.html
   PFLAG's transgender family site. Order or download a copy of the new edition of *Our Trans Children* at the following page:
   http://pflag.org/Our_Trans_Children_-_Intro.otc.0.html

http://www.transproud.org/
   Site for trans youth and parents.

Matthew's Place
www.MatthewsPlace.com
Features up-to-date national and LGBT news, advice columns, and an information hub for youth.

GenderPAC
http://www.gpac.org/
Works to promote freedom of gender expression.

Working with Transgender Youth
http://www.lambdalegal.org/take-action/tool-kits/getting-down-to-basics/trans-youth.html

The Trevor Project
1-866-4-U-TREVOR (1-866-488-7386)
Operates the nation's only 24/7 suicide and crisis prevention helpline for LGBT and questioning youth.

Laura's Playground
http://www.lauras-playground.com/transgender_transsexual_children.htm
Website with some content about transgender children.

Trans Youth Family Allies
http://www.imatyfa.org/

There are several national and regional Listservs for parents of gender-variant and transgender children, including those offered by the following organizations:

Children's National Medical Center, Washington, D.C.
For membership information, contact pgroup@cnmc.org

TransFamily of Cleveland
http://www.transfamily.org/emailist.htm

Books That Families May Find Useful
Mom, I Need to Be a Girl, by Just Evelyn
  Available online or in a PDF link through this site:
  http://ai.eecs.umich.edu/people/conway/TS/Evelyn/Evelyn.html

*Why Don't You Tell Them I'm a Boy? Raising a Gender-Nonconforming
  Child,* by Florence Dillon
  A mother's experience raising a transgender (FTM) son. Available online
  at: http://www.safeschoolscoalition.org/ whydontyoutellthem.pdf

Trans Forming Families: Real Stories About Transgendered Loved Ones, by
  Mary Boenke
  The classic first collection of stories from families of transgender
  children, available from PFLAG.

Transparent: Love, Family, and Living the T with Transgender Teenagers, by
  Cris Beam (Harvest paperback, 2008).
  A reporter's account of teaching and mentoring several transgirls
  in LA.

*Always My Child: A Parent's Guide to Understanding Your Gay, Lesbian,
  Bisexual, Transgendered or Questioning Son or Daughter,* by Kevin Jen-
  nings (Fireside, 2002).

*Transgender Emergence: Therapeutic Guidelines for Working With Gender-
  Variant People and Their Families,* by Arlene Istar Lev (Routledge,
  2004).

Transition and Beyond, Observations On Gender Identity, by Reid Vanderburgh (Q Press, 2007).

Social Services with Transgendered Youth, edited by Gerald P. Mallon, DSW
(Routledge, 2000).
Addresses the differences between male-to-female (MTF) and
female-to-male (FTM) individuals and offers suggestions to help
social workers and families learn more about the reality of transgendered persons' lives.

For Middle School Students / Teens
Luna, by Julie Anne Peters (Little, Brown, 2006).
Young adult novel about a family in which one child transitions from
male to female as a teenager.

Parrotfish, by Ellen Wittlinger (Simon & Schuster Children's Publishing, 2007).
Young adult novel about a transgendered high school junior who
knows she is a boy.

GLBTQ: The Survival Guide for Queer and Questioning Teens, by Kelly
Huegel (Free Spirit Publishing, 2003).
Written for teens beginning to question their sexual or gender iden-
tity and those interested in LGBT issues.

*Full Spectrum: A New Generation of Writing about Gay, Lesbian, Bisexual,
Transgender, Questioning, and Other Identities,* edited by David Levithan
and Billy Merrell (Knopf, 2006).

Chapter 5

Transition Decisions: When Should I Let My Child Live as Their Preferred Gender?

WHEN A PERSON CHANGES OUTWARDLY from one gender to another and lives in accordance with their gender identity, it is called going through transition, or *transitioning*. There is no rule of thumb for when a cross-gender child should be allowed to transition. But there usually comes a time when your child's suffering is so obvious that, despite your concerns, it is critically important to allow them to live in the world as they wish. Until then, how do you know? And how long after they tell you about their desire to live in accordance with their inner sense of gender is the right time to allow them this form of expression?

If only there were an easy answer to these questions. What is clear is that children who receive the support of their families have the best outcomes in terms of their future health and well-being. When contemplating options about allowing their child to transition, parents are afraid both for the physical safety of their child and of their child's rejection by others. The two most pressing questions parents have at this stage are "Will my child be safe if I let them do this?" and "Wouldn't it be better just to make them wait?" The most useful way of answering these questions is to first evaluate whether your child currently feels safe and satisfied, or if instead they are suffering. If your child is suffering, any dangers that await them as a transgender person may be easier to face than the dangers associated with their current depression.

The Process of Transition

When parents have time to observe their child's gender variance or transgender identity from a young age on, their level of acceptance has time to progress. A young child can only transition with the direct approval of their parents. In a sense, the parents and the child transition—together. Often the parent of a very young child takes a number of years to be sure that this cross-gender identity is not just a protracted phase.

Parents whose children announce their transgender status without warning feel the poignancy of loss and confusion much more acutely than those for whom the transition was a gradual evolution.

I did not see this coming at all, and was in a state of shock for some time. —Parent of a 20-year-old transwoman

Transgender children and other gender-variant children who want to express themselves grow tired of being misperceived, invalidated, and forced to wear clothes or present themselves in ways that feel unnatural, uncomfortable, and possibly embarrassing. Your child may have felt this way for a long time and not had the words to express it. Many older children and teens, by the time they tell you, may have been silently suffering for years. Your child may be one of the few to have just realized one day that they are transgender—likely from exposure to a transgender person, and it felt so right for them. Or, your child may have been trying to tell you this for some time, and only now are you hearing them.

Children are not transgender in order to rebel or to make your life harder for you. These children are brave and beautiful individuals. Their need to be themselves is greater than any other concern for them. Their desire to live out in the world within their natural gender expression, or in alignment with their gender identity, is the desire to live life authentically. When they tell you they are transgender, they are sharing with you that they are no longer able to live their life under learned gender pretense in order to reduce real or perceived humiliation, rejection, and persecution. They want your approval and continued love. They want you to love them for who they are.

The Risks of a Mixed Message

I tell my kindergartner that I know he's a girl. But that he can be a girl and a mommy when he grows up. For now, he will be a boy at school because people don't understand. —Parent of a 6-year-old transgender child

We let our teenage daughter know that it is completely fine with us that she wants to be a man. But she needs to wait until she has graduated from high school. Then she can start college as a man. —Parents of a transgender high school student

Telling your child that you are fine with who they are—but that they have to wait to live as who they truly are—gives them a powerful message, and it may not be the one you wish to impart. You are telling them that while they live with you they must stay hidden and keep their true identity to themselves. If you truly believe that your child is transgender, there is no reason why they should not live in accordance with their gender identity. The future is a distant concept to a child. If they cannot see that far ahead to the time when they can be themselves, you may be increasing the risk of your child leaving home, or committing suicide.

Living life as a transgender person is not an easy path to walk, but it is a truthful one. Every transgender child, teen, and adult we have met has felt that they gained tremendously by living life in accordance with their true gender identity. There is not a "right" time to outwardly change genders. Different moments have their benefits and drawbacks. If you really know your child is transgender and they want to transition to live in accordance with their true self, with your support, let them begin.

What Is the Appropriate Timeline?

Please be wary of any professional who tries to tell you that there is a correct time to allow your child to transition. This is not true; there is no "appropriate" timeline. Each family walks this path on their own, determining what is right given their unique set of circumstances.

> *The psychiatrist we saw after our son told us he was transgender and needed to live life as a girl told us that our son should wait six months before he dressed like a girl outside of the house. If we had enforced that rule, we would probably not have our child with us anymore, since telling us was his/her last resort before committing suicide. She was shocked when we didn't reject her. She thought we would reject her and she knew she couldn't live with that. She also knew she could not live another day as a boy. We thank God every day that we responded as we did. We would so much rather have a transgender child than no child at all. Anyway, three months was as long as she could wait to start living full-time as a girl. We had to move very fast. But we did it as a team. She got into therapy, we got into therapy, she saw an endocrinologist, we spoke with her teachers, we told our friends and family, she got electrolysis, we bought new clothes and makeup, we had her hair styled, and boom—out popped our daughter. They give you nine months for pregnancy. This was the accelerated version. Don't listen if someone gives you a timeline. Do whatever you need to do to keep your child alive.* —Parent of a 17-year-old trans daughter

What does seem to be safe to generalize is this: the younger the child when they assert their cross-gender nature and request to live in accordance with their inner gender identity, the longer the parents can wait. That is, the longer the child can get by with a more ambiguous gender state.

> For quite a few months we referred to our child as "our cute lit-tle big-boy, she is such a kind child." In other words, we referred to our child as our "son" and as a "boy," but could not change the pronouns! People probably thought we were really weird, but since our child was in preschool they were pretty forgiving. I can-not possibly imagine doing the same thing and having it work for our child or for other people if we did this now when our child is 10, or at 14! That was a luxury I am grateful for. In a way we had more time because we had more control over our young child than we would over an older child. —Parent of a 10-year-old transboy

If your child is about to enter puberty or is already in puberty, the desire to transition takes on a whole new meaning and is accompanied by a much stronger sense of urgency than when your child is young. There are impending body changes to deal with. Please read Chapter 8, Medical Issues for Transgender Children, thoroughly to help you under-stand the options you have for "buying time." There are medications available that you can give your child now to put their pubertal changes on hold while you figure out exactly what is happening. It is important not to rush into making permanent physical changes. But it is also impor-tant to consider pressing the Pause button on your child's natural phys-ical adolescent development.

Please find the support of a therapist who can help you and your family navigate this important time of life. You all should proceed with your eyes wide open, educated about the choices you are making and the options available to you.

Parents need to strive to find a balance that works for everyone in the family. Of course, your child or teen has a much different perspective on time than you do as an adult. Sometimes you can hold the reins and maintain a pace that feels manageable to you. However, if your child waited until they were severely distressed before informing you, you may not have as much time as you would prefer to fully process this information and determine the appropriate course of action. In such a case it can feel as if you are doing everything you can to catch up with a train that is already moving. Although it may seem unbearably fast in the beginning, this whirlwind feeling will abate and your life will settle down again. It may take some time, but it will happen.

If you are in support of your child transitioning, it is best to gain the full support of all legal parents, if at all possible, before allowing the child to begin a gender transition. That is the safest way to do it, from a legal standpoint. If that is not possible, you may want to consult with a lawyer about the consequences of proceeding without the support of all parents. Also read Chapter 9, Legal Issues to Consider.

How Do We Begin?

Once again, there is no formula for a successful transition. Usually, when a child is young, the family begins by allowing the child greater freedom with the social markers of gender. Perhaps they first let the child choose their own hairstyle and length, and then later allow the same freedom with clothing. Many families of young children allow their child to present themselves as their inner gender but hold on to their birth name and pronouns for a little longer.

If you have an older child who wants to transition, outward appearances often predate any announcement from your child. Families handle things differently from there. Some let their child "try on" living as a boy or a girl outside of school.

Other families decide to work hand in hand with their school about the best time to transition. Supportive schools often want a little time to prepare and educate their staff so that the child can receive support at school during this tender time. When the school is ready, the child is allowed to dress and present themselves as they choose. Based on her work at Gender Spectrum, Stephanie feels strongly that your child will have the greatest success if the school has been trained and the students have been educated about gender diversity prior to your child's transition.

Other families allow the child to self-direct the process. Just be clear that in taking this approach it is not your hope that your child will try to transition and fail. If you realize that you are hoping for that outcome, please stop and find a way to change the arrangement so that you can be more supportive of your child.

Going through transition is a very exciting and trying time for everyone close to the transitioning child. However, it is essential to keep in mind that your child is the one who needs parental support. It is your job as a parent to search outside the home for the support you need personally during this time.

Temporarily Using No Pronouns

What if your child asks you to allow them to live in accordance with their gender identity but you are not ready to do so? Many families try to honor their young child's request to live as their inner gender by using gender-neutral language, or by repeating their child's name rather than use pronouns at all (for example, "Jenny wants to go to the movies with friends" or "Jenny wants to go the movies with Jenny's friends"). These families may not be ready to change pronouns, but they also do not want to refer to their child in a way that makes their child uncomfortable. This is a very awkward phase. But it is valuable, too. When you try to go even a day without using pronouns, you can see how much gender informs our daily speech.

We went a whole year of our lives—when our child was 5 years old—trying not to use any pronouns. Our trans daughter had told us she was a girl for three years at that point. We simply did not believe at that time that kids should be able to change their gender. We wanted her to be a girl-boy. This didn't work for her. We struck a deal that we would not refer to her as a boy to anyone that we did not know. It was that, or have endless sorrowful tantrums wherever we went. So we learned to speak without pronouns. I cannot tell you what a relief it was when we finally agreed to change pronouns and we could just speak freely again. But let me tell you, it gave both of us a lot more sympathy for children who do not feel like they are either gender. Our language boxes people in, right from the start. —Parent of an 8-year-old transgirl*

Changing Pronouns and Respect for Gender

Changing your child's name and pronouns feels like the final frontier for many parents. It is a scary step, particularly since it feels like full acceptance of your child's cross-gender status. The ramifications seem enormous. Nonetheless, if your child requests that you change their pronouns, it is essential to respond to their request in an effective and supportive manner as soon as possible. This will minimize any negative impact your initial responses may have had on your child.

When our 3-year-old sat with us at the dinner table and told us we were breaking her heart by not calling her "him," we knew the time had come. We had to take the leap of faith. What ultimately helped me the most (besides the clear plea from my child) was when I realized that I wasn't committing for life. I was just committing to honoring my child right now. This made it possible for me. Just as she said she was a boy, then one day she may say she's a girl. All she was asking was for a name and pronoun shift. Why did it feel

like the whole world was changing? That was so long ago. I have
compassion for myself when I look back and realize how hard this
was for me at the time—but it does seem silly that it felt like such
a big deal. —Parent of a 9-year-old transboy

Indeed, if your child is cross-gender, there will come a time when a formal social transition is the desired course of action, and it should therefore be honored. Many parents temporarily use their child's new pronoun in their presence but the old pronoun when apart from them, as a way of holding on to their old child a little longer. Usually after a few weeks to a few months, this becomes a thing of the past, and parents grow more comfortable referring to their child by their new pronoun. Sometimes they slip and use the old pronoun—but this is usually from force of habit rather than lack of support. Communicating this distinction to your child will help them be forgiving of your mistakes.

In some families, one parent makes the change before the other is ready. Although this may seem confusing, many children actually feel the support of the acknowledging parent and come to understand the reluctance of the other parent. Of course, the main problem in this situation is what happens in public: if one parent uses *he* and the other *she,* heads may turn.

Another issue comes up when parents refer to their child by their chosen gender pronoun in the present tense, but use the old pronoun when referring to events in the past. This crossed use of pronouns can work fine among family and understanding company. But with those who may not know the gender history of your child, you may be reticent to refer to the past at all for fear of letting something slip.

For most parents of transgender children and teens, there is an awkward phase of adjustment in all these matters. This period can range from several months to several years. Then, one day, you look back and realize everything is now completely normalized.

Our youngest child decided he would be the pronoun police. Every
time we used the wrong pronoun he collected a dime from us. This

was a way he could feel included, and we were able to have some-
one keeping us in check. —Parent of a 12-year-old transboy

We use feminine pronouns except when we slip up—perhaps
about half of the time. —Parent of a 20-year-old cross-gender
daughter

He wanted to be called a girl for a while, but now we seem to have
settled back on using male pronouns again. We realize this might
well change again in the future. —Parent of a 5-year-old gender-
fluid boy

I realized that when I kept calling my newly identified son "she" to
others I was actually confusing them. I would say she, but expect
them to change it to he. I didn't want to let go of my daughter. I was
so sad and confused. But when I used he, my friends and everyone
around me used he. It was as if they were looking to me for the appro-
priate response. I wanted someone else to lead me, but I had to do it
myself. It was a hard couple of months. I am used to it now. But I still
look at photos of my little daughter. Now I have a teenage son and will
probably have a son for the rest of my life. But my daughter still lives
with me, too. In my heart. —Parent of a transgender teenager

Making Space for Your Child's Feelings about You as a Parent

Each child experiences differing levels of angst about their gender variance, and angst in how to share this reality with family. Although they
may be strong in the knowledge that they are transgender, they may not
feel pride in who they are. Transgender people are so marginalized, mis-
understood, and misrepresented that your child may have internalized
a lot of shame about who they are. Much as you may naturally be
focused on your own emotional experience, it is vital to remember that
your child has a unique emotional experience of their own.

Remind yourself, and your child, that they are still the same person inside—even after they transition or begin to present differently. You still share the same experiences and memories. They are still your child, trusting you to be there for them. They are likely afraid that you will reject them. Many transgender people experience a sense of grief alongside their excitement at the time of transition. This is completely normal. A part of them is going away so that a new part can emerge.

It is extremely rare that a parent will know what to say and how to express perfect comfort at finding out that their child is transgender. Your child or teen will likely have difficulty coming to terms with your parental reaction—they may experience grief and anger as they realize that you are not the ideal parent, one who immediately accepts and understands them. Whatever degree of support you show for your child's gender identity, they may need to share with you each and every way they have felt unsupported by you over the years. This can be a painful process for parent and child, holding their hurt with them— knowing all the while you were doing the best you could. Your child may be in a rush for you to assist them in getting medical treatment to change their body, and may be furious at you for taking the time to explore the options first. Again, this is normal. Together you will weather the emotional storms.

Be Brave

The time of transition may be the hardest time of your parenthood. If you can make it through this stage maintaining a strong and connected relationship with your child, you will be a much stronger family in the end. Do everything within your power to stay connected to your child and to your spouse or partner, if you have one. Take the time to include all siblings right from the start. When you waver and feel afraid, remember that you are not alone—thousands of families face these very same decisions. When in doubt, reach out. Go to a Listserv, plan to attend a gathering such as the Gender Spectrum Family Conference, and get connected to other families who are raising transgender children. It takes courage to follow the path of love. As a child transitions, so does a parent. Be brave, and know you will go forward in this journey together.

Chapter 6

Disclosure: Whom to Tell, How, Why, and When

WHEN YOU ARE RAISING a gender-variant or transgender child or teenager, the issue of disclosure is a major one. Parents need to decide whom to talk to about their children, when to share information, when not to say anything, the differences between privacy and secrecy, who gets to decide who knows and who doesn't, and how to respond to negative reactions. Additionally, the child (and their siblings) must be prepared for the uneducated or biased reactions of others.

Most of these decisions will be made on the fly. Sometimes you will make choices that feel good, and sometimes you will end up having made a choice that does not feel good. That is all too often how we learn. In this chapter we explore how to find the courage to speak confidently about your child. We end the chapter with a list of questions people commonly ask about gender-variant and transgender children, and we provide some quick responses that both educate and make clear the issue is not up for extended discussion. Once you grow more confident speaking about gender, you will find the answers that work best for you and your family.

Finding Courage and Learning the Language

The more you learn to speak with confidence and pride about your child, the easier it will be for others to accept your child and your parenting choices. People look to you, as the child's parents, for their lead in how to respond or react. If you are secure in your support of your child, you will communicate it in your words, tone, facial expression, and body language. This sense of comfort comes with time and practice.

Finding Your Voice

There are a number of things that you can do to actively acquire a greater sense of confidence in your speech and communication about this subject. The first is to spend time exploring what it is you are afraid of when you think about speaking freely about your child. For most parents it is the fear of a negative response combined with the concern that they may not be doing the right thing by letting their child naturally express themselves.

> *I remember in those first few years I was so concerned with what others thought about me. This whole process of raising Gavi has made me have to grow up. I am now one hundred percent secure in the fact that what matters is my love and support of my child, not my fear of what others will think about me. It is so liberating! This new attitude has helped me enormously in all parts of my life.* —Parent of a 7-year-old transgirl

Being around other parents who share the challenge of communicating confidently about their gender-variant or transgender child can boost your self-assurance. Indeed, the value of spending time with other families with a gender-variant or transgender child cannot be overemphasized. It will provide you with the certainty that you are not alone. It can also give you a safe forum for expressing your fears and concerns.

After spending time with other parents, you feel the strength in numbers behind you when you speak. It can reassure you that you are not parenting in a vacuum, that many other parents face the same choices and challenges as you. Meeting other parents with gender-variant children can be highly reassuring, and will provide you with the information necessary to speak confidently about your child. For example, if someone questions your choices, it helps to be able to say, "At the conference I attended for families with gender-variant and transgender children, we learned about the current research regarding the most effective parenting practices for our children. One of the points that was stressed was just how important it is for all members of a child's family to be as supportive as possible."

The second thing that can dramatically help you feel more confident when speaking about your child is to practice. Practice is invaluable when it comes to trying out what to say about your child to others. It can really pay to imagine yourself in various situations and role-play with a friend, partner, or your therapist. Practice responses to the most common questions you receive. Ask for reflection from your practice partner: Does your response make sense? Is it clear? Are you defensive? What is your body language communicating?

Once you have mastered responses to the most common questions, start developing responses to the questions you are most afraid of answering. Practice responses to hostile confrontations. Imagine your worst-case scenarios, and practice, practice, practice! As silly as this technique may sound, it can make all the difference in securing your confidence.

If you are nervous about speaking about your child's gender, it can seem less overwhelming to divide the people you need to talk to into categories, such as these:

- Family
- Friends—yours and your child's
- Neighbors
- Co-workers
- Spiritual communities
- School/camp/classes
- Strangers or causal acquaintances

I used to be terrified and tongue-tied whenever someone would ask about my daughter. Finally my husband and I spent an entire night practicing responses. We actually videotaped ourselves and watched our responses. Together, we learned what were the easiest and clearest ways to speak about our situation to others. The most important thing we realized is that we have nothing to apologize for, and nothing to be embarrassed about. When we eliminated that from our speech we became a lot more confident. We recommend that anyone with a transgender child practice, practice, practice. It helps tremendously with your shame. —Parent of a 10-year-old transboy

The Educational Aspect of Disclosure

Every time you tell someone about your child's gender variance there is an excellent chance that you will find yourself educating them. This is especially true with close friends and neighbors, who will see your child frequently and be very curious. However, there is a time and place for this kind of education. You may feel quite burdened by the responsibility to educate others just so they can embrace and welcome your child. We discuss the need for school-facilitated parent education events on gender diversity in Chapter 7, The Educational System and Your Family. In your daily life it can be important to set boundaries for yourself and your child.

For example, if someone approaches you and it's clear they want to chat with you about your child, you can always nicely—yet firmly—deflect the conversation. One way to do this is by saying something like "I would be happy to talk to you more about this and answer your questions, but here at the soccer game probably isn't the best time. If you want to get together for coffee, we could spend more time talking about this."

One family we know has made business cards with resource information to hand out to people. Our friend says: "There is so much to learn about this subject. As you can imagine, I could spend my life educating others about my child instead of raising her! So I simply say, 'Here's a card showing how you can get more information. Why don't you check out these resources? If you still have remaining questions, just ask!' "

Discussing Your Child with Your Family

All our relatives responded in a warm and welcoming way. My mother immediately bought my daughter a charm bracelet, and a cousin sent a big case of makeup upon receiving our disclosure email. —Parent of a 20-year-old transwoman

Most of our relatives have been great. They tell everyone about my kid because they feel he is so special and they want to help educate others. The right-wing Christian members of the extended family know that if they want peace they will accept this or be quiet, or they will have a fight on their hands. I just have to be careful with my ex-husband's side of the family. —Parent of a 7-year-old transboy

My one regret about how we handled things is that I think we should have told my family sooner rather than holding off for two years. —Parent of a 26-year-old transwoman

As hard as it may be for you as a parent to come to terms with the gender variance your child is expressing, it can be even more difficult to try to figure out how to share this with extended family members. It's important to realize that even in the most loving of families, people need time to change long-held beliefs. So while it may seem tempting to try to hide this aspect of their child until it is all figured out, this approach will not necessarily serve you. Other people in your life may need time to come along on this journey with you. Those you are close to and want to continue having strong relationships with deserve the time to adjust to the ideas you are presenting—you may find that they become your staunchest allies if you afford them that opportunity. Remember that you cannot rush anyone's thought process on this subject, even if you really need their immediate love and support.

There are ways to encourage the desired responses from your family members. Once again, this has to do with your delivery and what it is you are asking for. Most people, when told what they are being asked to do, respond with that in mind. If you do not offer them guidance, it becomes more of a free-for-all, and you decrease the likelihood of getting the response you want.

Most family members can be divided into two categories: those who are especially close to you, and extended family members who are not as close. We feel that the people who are closest to you should be included in the disclosure right from the start, usually in one-on-one conversations.

In larger families, and for family members who are not as close, many people have found that sending out a letter works well. A letter can be an extremely effective form of communication, and can be sent to everyone in the family at the same time. In a letter you have a chance to say your truth before answering any questions, and without having to hear a person's initial response. Initial responses are often completely unguarded and inflamed; perspectives usually change after some reflection. A mass communication makes it easier for you, as coping with everyone's initial responses is emotionally draining—especially since not only is your child being called into question, but often your parenting as well.

It is best to send a letter via postal mail rather than a mass email communication to the whole clan. That way, it cannot be deleted by mistake, forwarded to others without your permission, or used as a subject of endless discussion between family members online. Especially in this age of electronic communication, sending a formal letter in the mail also carries more weight—something to be taken seriously and considered carefully.

Here is a sample disclosure letter:

Dear (Family member),

We have some big news to announce. Our child, Jeremy, has recently shared with us that he no longer feels like he is a boy. In fact, we have learned that the child we thought was our son is actually our daughter. Through careful self-exploration, family talks, and therapy, we have all come to understand the truth of this for her. So we are proud to announce that we all have a new family member! Jenny, as is her name now, is living full-time as a girl. She is very happy about this and so are we. We are so proud of our daughter for having the courage to share with us her deepest truth. As you are all an important part of our lives, we wanted to be able to share this with you as well.

We know that this may be confusing for some of you. It certainly was for us in the beginning. However, there is a lot of information available about transgender people—we would like to invite you to explore some of these materials. There are organizations with helpful websites, such as Parents and Friends of Lesbians and Gays (PFLAG). And as you may even be aware, there has been an increasing amount of television coverage on this subject over the last few years, including specials on *20/20* with Barbara Walters, and on *Oprah*.

We request that you welcome Jenny fully as part of our family. Please only refer to her by female pronouns and by her name, Jenny. Despite any personal feelings you may have about our decision, we expect that you will be fully respectful of Jenny.

If you are no longer able to treat our child with complete respect, then we will decline further contact until that changes.

Our love and support for Jenny is complete. We hope yours
will be too.

A letter such as this can be adapted easily to your situation. Whether
you have a boy who wears dresses and you want to avoid negative comments, questions, or looks, or your child feels they are neither a boy nor
a girl, or your child is like any of the others you see reflected in this book,
a letter can be a great help with your disclosure to family members.

Senior Family Members

Many families are afraid of how the oldest members of the family will
respond to their gender-variant child or transgender child. Some fear the
rejection of these family members. While that outcome is possible, many
families have reported that they were amazed that the 92-year-old great-
grandmother was the most understanding of any relative. Or the 85-
year-old grandfather who just smiled and said, "That's all right with me,
son. If you want to wear a dress, go ahead. Life is too precious to let others tell you what to wear!"

This open-mindedness of seniors may come from having lived a long
life, and learning that love is more important than pretext. It also may
come from the fact that the older generation often has a lot more exposure to daytime television, which actually covers many transgender
issues. There have been numerous, generally well-presented, talk shows
devoted to transgender children. So older folks may have greater exposure to issues about transgender children than many people your own
age, who, after all, have much less time to watch daytime television.

*We were so nervous when my trans teen, David, was going to tell
my parents that he is now a boy. They had done OK a few years
prior when he said he was a lesbian, but we were really not sure
how they would react this time. This seemed so much more risky.
We debated in private about whether or not to tell them ahead of*

time. Our son asked us not to. We decided to follow his wishes. Well, the day came, and we all went over there. He blurted it out within the first five minutes of arriving. They were confused and asked him to slow down and tell them what exactly he was saying. I suggested we move into the living room and sit down and talk for a while. On the way in there I grabbed my son in the hall and told him to just speak slowly and give them a chance. I explained they didn't understand, and that is different than rejection. We spent the next hour talking about what was going on for David. By the end of the talk each of the grandparents had told David that they love him no matter what. My dad was pretty confused and didn't say much. But he gave David a big hug. My mom was more verbal. She was very chatty. I could tell she was scared that she would do the wrong thing.

My parents called me that night and were pretty upset. Not upset because David was transgender. They were upset that I hadn't given them time to prepare for how to respond. They felt put on the spot. They requested that in the future I tell them these things first. I explained about David's wishes. And his fear that if they rejected him, he might never see them again. By telling them himself, he would at least get a chance to say good-bye. They both got silent and said they would never reject their grandchild. We ended on a good note and all has been fine since then. Sometimes they mix up his name and pronouns. But sometimes they call me by my sister's name or my brother's name. So David knows this is not personal. —Parent of an 18-year-old transboy

If Your Family Rejects or Ridicules Your Child

I have told many people, but not some of my family. They are a very conservative right-wing group, and I fear they will not be accepting of this. —Parent of an 18-year-old transgirl

We have told people who don't understand that we believe they are
responding to their own fears and anxieties rather than our child
or us. We have said that if you wish to criticize, please do so from
an informed position. If you are responding from emotion, find
out what is creating that feeling before you express what you think.
—Parent of a 20-year-old transwoman

Sometimes family members are very critical of the choices you make in support of your child's gender variance. They can let you know this in so many ways. They might even tease and ridicule your children. This should not be tolerated; allowing this form of rejection to continue gives your child a very strong, and damaging, message. Every child needs to know that they are the most important thing in your life and that you will honor and protect them. By allowing your family to ridicule them, you show them that they are not worth protecting.

On the other hand, telling a family member to stop can feel scary even when you know it is the right thing to do. Their ridicule may be directed only at you, away from your child's presence. In any case, be very direct in your response. "I love my child unconditionally. I will not tolerate it if you continue to be critical of her and the parenting choices we are making. If you are unable to support her and our parenting, we will stop having contact until that can change."

Such statements can be so very hard to make, yet it is critical to do so. Many parents feel that it wouldn't be fair to their other children to lose having Aunt Suzy, or Grandpa, in their lives because of the gender-variant sibling. But if you do not stick up for your child, all your children will take note. Sticking up for your child may make the others angry and frustrated, but they will respect you. They will know that you will stand up for them as well, no matter who they become.

Please remember that even if your immediate family must stop seeing other family members for a while, it does not have to be permanent. People change and grow. Many people who are estranged from certain family members over this issue continue to send them yearly letters or holiday cards, letting them know through these overtures that they are welcome back into their lives if they choose to be respectful.

Examining the Homophobia of Your Extended Family

There is a connection between people's attitudes toward gay people and their attitudes toward gender-nonconforming people. Many people come from families where making jokes about gay people is normal; they sneer or make derogatory, homophobic comments when someone who does not fit the expected gender presentation walks by. It is common for kids to be told not to walk like they are gay, throw like they are gay, and so on. When someone says something stupid, people say, "That's so gay." Remarks and expressions like these are unfortunately commonplace in daily life.

Gender-variant children of all ages are often described as being gay. Parents who allow their gender-nonconforming children to express themselves naturally are blamed for supporting the "gay agenda." There is no "gay agenda." Anyone who invokes that myth is someone who resists equal rights for all people.

In raising gender-variant children, the healthiest approach is to adopt a philosophy of love. If you love, accept, and value your child and you model kindness and respect for all, then your child will know that bigotry has no place. This is an easy way to communicate your philosophy to others as well. Rather than engaging in a debate that may leave both sides feeling disconnected from each other, many people find it easiest to say something like this: "Please do not speak badly about gay people. We are teaching our children not to judge others, and to accept everyone with love." Or this: "We practice love and kindness. I would prefer that you refrain from negative comments about any group of people when you are in my presence."

If you want to respond more specifically about your child, you can say this: "My child may or may not be gay. It does not matter to us, because we will love and accept him regardless. We will not tolerate negative comments about our child or judgments about our parenting." Although it can be challenging to speak up this way in the face of bigotry, it sends an important message to your child. When your child witnesses you standing up for love and acceptance, their self-esteem becomes more secure.

Secrecy versus Privacy

Every family decides whether to tell people that their child is transgender. There is no "right" way to do this. However, there is a lot to think about. The central issue is this: Who makes the decisions about whether to tell people and whom to tell? Some people feel that their child should decide, while others feel that this is a parental decision. People have very different opinions about whether they are obliged to tell anyone at all. The issue of disclosure brings up an ethical issue as well. Those who feel biological sex is a matter of personal privacy are outraged by the idea that disclosure should be an obligation. Those who feel an obligation to disclose are concerned by those who keep the matter private. You will need to examine what feels right for you and your family.

The Argument for Telling Everyone

Some parents feel that everyone in their child's life should know and deserves to know that their child is transgender. They feel that this reduces the likelihood that their child will internalize shame. Keeping the issue aboveboard ensures that no one feels betrayed by not having been told. Parents who choose full disclosure also welcome the decreased need to self-censor around others. For these families, not sharing this information freely feels like keeping a secret.

This gets tricky only when the child asks for privacy and the parents proceed on the basis that full disclosure is the way to approach it. The child is then continually exposed against their will. Although this may look like full support, there is a significant discrepancy between what the child feels as support and what the parents feel is best for the child.

In defense of personal privacy, transgender teens have made this argument: "If the doctor had messed up on my circumcision and cut off half my penis, would you feel compelled to tell everyone I meet? Would it be a secret if I didn't tell them, or would you respect my need for privacy?" In contrast, other teens have been highly appreciative that their parents made the decision for them.

The Argument for Letting Your Child Decide Who Knows

If a child prefers to be private about their biological sex, many parents agree to go along with that choice. In these families, the child is in control of who is aware of their genital status. These parents might encourage their child to come out to certain people about being transgender. Or the parents and child might agree together on who should know and whom it will be the child's choice to tell or not tell.

The potential problem with this approach is that it gets harder to reveal this information in the future to people you already know. Your child may have a greater fear of rejection, since there is already an established relationship and it is unknown how the person will respond. As a result, the child may internalize some shame around this and grow fearful of being found out.

> I envy the kids who only figure out they are trans when they are older. Then everyone has to know. They don't decide to tell people, people just know because they make their change at school. Of course they probably get a lot of teasing and lose a lot of friends. So I wouldn't like that part. That's why I don't tell people now. They just wouldn't understand. —8-year-old transboy

Are You Encouraging Shame If You Allow Your Child to Stay Private?
In an ideal world, no one would feel they had to keep this kind of information private. However, we are not there now. The people we have met who do not freely share this information with everyone are not ashamed about being transgender. Far from it. Rather, they are weighing the risks of disclosure against the risks of maintaining people's assumptions. They are making daily assessments about the impact of disclosure at a given time.

Revealing this level of personal information is something that needs to be navigated. Transgender children from a very early age learn to read safety in a situation and use this information to decide how much to reveal, and how much to keep private. Privacy can develop into shame if the need for privacy is driven by the parents—the communication to the child is that there is a secret to keep. Secrets breed shame. However, if the desire for privacy comes from the child, and the parents encourage the child to test the waters of self-disclosure when it feels right, because there is nothing to be ashamed of, the child is much less likely to choose privacy due to internalized shame.

Many parents grapple with whether to tell their children's playmates. This decision will depend on what your community is like, your child's age, your child's playmates, the play date situation (water parks and sleepovers, for example, will be more complicated than just an hour of playing with toys in your house), and whether your child has already transitioned. You will have to weigh these factors and decide whether to make a disclosure, and when, on a case-by-case basis.

Some transgender children choose to disclose selectively. For example, they do not disclose that they are transgender to their fellow classmates, but they may tell the school nurse or certain teachers. Or they tell close family friends, but not the kids on their soccer team. They may tell friends who live out of town, but not their classmates. Kids are able to monitor reactions, and the potential reactions, of others to assess the risks of disclosure. It seems like a lot of work, and it is. But for some it is safer to hold that control. At least for as long as it lasts.

I would tell my best friend at school. But I know she can't keep a secret. I wouldn't want her to feel pressured to keep it private. I am not ready for everyone to know. I'm thinking I will tell kids when I am older. I have told lots of adults and some kids who don't live around here. Everyone has been fine. But I don't want the kids at school to look at me differently than they look at me now. —10-year-old transgirl

The Natural Sifting of Your Adult Friends

If you have a gender-variant child, you come to learn pretty quickly which of your adult friends are going to stay in your life and who is more likely to drift away. This is a deep reality check. Friends tend to fall on one side of the fence or the other: accepting and supportive or confused and rejecting. Some friends you are already close to will walk with you on this journey. You will be able to confide in them about your initial questions, concerns, and doubts. As time progresses and things become clearer, together you can move into acceptance and the full support of your child. These friends will stay with you through the long haul. Those who naturally fall away are people you do not need in your life. The loss may be quite poignant, especially at the time. Rejection by those we love always hurts.

I started with my most trusted and deepest friends. I eventually sent an announcement letter to our neighbors. Most people have been wonderfully supportive. It's been nearly nine months now and I have adopted the attitude that if I treat this with shame or embarrassment, I am perpetuating the problem that we have in society. —Parent of a 20-year-old transwoman

If they can't deal with this, it tells me something about them. —Parent of a gender-variant 10-year-old girl

New Adult Friends

Then there is the question of new friends—people who may not even know your child, perhaps the parents of one of your other children's friends. Do you owe them an explanation? Will they understand if you tell them? What if you tell them only much later and lose their trust because they feel you were hiding this from them? These are tough questions. It is sometimes easier if your child is obviously gender-variant, as it comes up naturally. However, if your child is transgender and living in accordance with their gender identity, people have no way of knowing unless you or your child, or someone else, tells them.

> *I have a new friend. We are getting closer. We spend time with our younger children together. She has met my older (trans) child, but she does not know he is trans. I don't feel the need to tell her. I am very clear that she may feel like I don't trust her when I do tell her. But I do not know her well enough to tell her or ask her not to talk about it to other people we know in common. My trans child is private about his transgender status. He likes to have control over who knows and who doesn't. We respect that. But it does get complicated.* —Parent of a 15-year-old transboy

> *I find I either have to educate and bring along my friends in this journey with our son's gender-fluid nature—or they just fall away.* —Parent of a 9-year-old gender-variant child

Disclosure to Others

Neighbors

Everyone tends tend to worry about what the neighbors think about everything. Usually, the neighbors are too busy with their own problems to care much about anyone else's. But as with other people in your life who see a transition, or unexpected gender variance, in your child, neighbors may eventually ask for some explanation. It is up to you to decide whether to tell them and how much information to share. Gossip will spread regardless, as it does in any neighborhood about everyone.

Co-workers

Many workplace environments foster close friendships. From the photos in your cubicle to chatter in the lunchroom or over after-work drinks, our co-workers usually learn a lot about us. As a parent, you will have to decide how much of your child's personal life comes through the door with you each day at work. While you may find great support from your co-workers for life's big changes, you also need to remember that the workplace is a professional space, and drama of any kind is best left at home. If you don't want the whole office to know your business, it is often best not to tell anyone private news that should not be repeated. That said, many parents have found a trusted co-worker to be a good starting point for disclosure about their child.

> It was so hard to talk about in the beginning. I was in shock. I remember how I felt, saying the words the first time to a trusted co-worker. It was so hard to do. We both cried. But then I realized that after I spoke the words, the world did not come crashing down. —Parent of a 20-year-old transwoman

> The only thing I would have done differently, when I look back, is that I would have confronted the person at my workplace who got defensive about my child, rather than accommodating her defensiveness. —Parent of a 28-year-old transwoman

People You Have Just Met

When you have a young child who is gender-variant or transgender, you often have to tell people before you've even begun a friendship with them. This can be awkward, as you are sharing very personal information before you really know them. For example, your child is in kindergarten and has been invited to go swimming with a new friend after school. If your child is transgender and the new parent does not know, you cannot simply leave them to find out on their own when your child changes into a bathing suit. So you must decide whether to tell them, or make up an excuse for why your child can't swim with them, or invite yourself along. It is an awkward burden that can lead to uncomfortable dynamics with new people. Keep practicing new ways to navigate this.

Strangers

Recently we have decided it's no one's business what is between my kid's legs. —Parent of a 7-year-old transboy

Many, many families with gender-variant and transgender children treat strangers differently from anyone else in their lives in regard to whether or not to disclose. If someone at the grocery store perceives your son to be a girl, do you correct them? Our general advice to you on this point is to let your child take the lead with unknown people you will not likely encounter again. This gives your child a greater sense of control, and can protect them from negative reactions from people they do not even know. It is important not to give your child the message that there is something wrong with them that shouldn't be spoken about. And it is important for your child to feel safe moving about in the world.

Situations Where No One Knows
There are some unique opportunities and benefits to cultivating environments where your child has the option of not having to challenge other people's perceptions. It can give your child a sense of respite and relief.

For example, Jesse, who is 9, has a female gender presentation and gender identity. She is biologically male. She has recently started to use female pronouns, and her parents are supportive of her emerging transgender identity. At school, the kids have followed her progression from gender fluidity to a more stable sense of gender. Some kids call her "she" and others "he." This has been the case for a year or so. Jesse would prefer that they all switch to "she" but she knows it will take time. Summer is approaching and Jesse wants the opportunity to attend a camp without the other staff or campers knowing she is biologically male.

Her parents struggle with this. Up to this point, they have always been out in the open about Jesse's gender-fluid status. However, now that she is strongly cross-gender, it no longer seems clear what to do. They don't want her to keep a secret, and yet they want to honor her desire to just be a regular kid at camp. After much discussion they decide to let her go to camp as female without disclosing her transgender status. She changes in the restroom, so there is no accidental disclosure in the changing room. Jesse has the liberating experience of just getting to be one of the girls.

In situations like these, parents can try out their child's assertion that they are truly transgender. This can be very beneficial. After such an experience, some parents realize that it would be best for their child to switch schools and start again, undisclosed. Sometimes the burden of being out to everyone is too big, especially if it is in an environment that is not fully supportive. This kind of "try it out" opportunity can allow both parent and child to reflect on different options.

Running Into Someone You Know
Every parent handles this situation differently. Some use the opportunity to practice on-the-fly disclosure about their child. When you bump into someone you rarely see, you can see how they respond without taking a great risk. It can also be a good way to monitor how you react to their response.

We were shopping in the store when a parent from my oldest daughter's old swim team bumped into us. It was great to see her. We started to chat. She asked about the younger kids. She hadn't seen our trans child since he was still a girl. And there he was with us, completely unrecognizable. He was mortified when she asked about him. I just rolled with it and said, "Judith? Oh, yeah, you haven't seen us for a while. Judith changed his name to Edward, and here he is." She looked confused and said, "Oh, Edward ... I haven't seen you since you were a little baby." We did not say anything directly about the fact that he used to be a girl. We just said our good-byes and went on. —Parent of a 14-year-old transboy

I just bit the bullet and told the guys on the job that my teenage daughter is transgender. I did it in a way that showed my support for her AND let them know that if they had a problem with it we were going to have to take it outside. What surprised me the most was that within the week, two other guys shared that they had teens that were gay. Sometimes it pays to just put it out there. —Parent of a 16-year-old transboy

Cultural, Religious, Ethnic, and Racial Influences

Every community has different expectations about gender and gender roles. Every community also has different expectations about what you discuss and what you don't. So gender-variant and transgender children are a much bigger transgression for some religious or ethnic communities than for others. This can weigh heavily on the discussion of whether or not to disclose, especially when your religious or ethnic community is a main source of your strength and comfort.

It can be helpful to take stock of your community influences. List the overt communications about sexual orientation and gender identity, and the understood beliefs about LGBT people. Then you can identify people you perceive as "safe" within your various communities.

Approach these people first for support and ideas on how to talk to others in the community.

Remember that your child deserves love and respect and you have a right to expect and demand it. But that is easier said than done, especially if what you are asking is well beyond the comfort zone of the general community. Remember, there are LGBT people in every religious, racial, and ethnic community. It may require turning to new support systems to find them, but they are there. People may be more closeted or private about this than you, but with some sensitive exploration you will find others in your community who are more tolerant of your family. In the process of supporting your child you may lose important people in your life, but more than likely you will also gain some important new people to replace them.

Here are some quotes from other parents on this topic:

- "I am a Christian. But when religious people have a problem with my child I tell them we are all God's children."
- "You can have your own personal beliefs—but don't show disapproval around me."
- "I am very strongly against any church or leader of a church who promotes discrimination or hate. We found a new place to go to church by going online and searching for welcoming churches. Any church that can promote the idea of all being welcome is probably OK."
- "God makes no mistakes."
- "I told my great-aunt. She's the matriarch in the family. When she accepted that our son is gender-fluid, everyone accepted it."

Shunning

Many families fear being shunned from their community because of their gender-variant or transgender child. Or they fear that their child will be shunned at school or in other arenas of their life. First, let us reassure you that there are very few reports of this actually having happened. People have definitely felt driven out of their churches, and some people have certainly had to dissociate from their families of origin. But only rarely do we hear about a family being socially shunned within their community for raising a gender-variant or transgender child.

We have heard of parents, seeking a solution, who have sent their children to other states to live with family, or even with welcoming strangers, if a child was unexpectedly outed and became unsafe at home. Other families in such a situation waited awhile to see if things were going to settle down first before deciding they would have to move. When they moved, it was to a more liberal area where they were not as worried about their child's safety. For a fictional take on this, watch the charming Belgian film *Ma Vie en Rose,* about a young gender-variant boy whose family moves to a new town, where they find a much more welcoming environment.

Actual shunning may not have to occur to motivate a family to move—just the promise of a fresh start elsewhere.

> *We moved from our home, due to our child's discomfort in coming out in our former small town, so she could finish high school elsewhere, and then we bought a new home an hour away.* —Parent of a 20-year-old transwoman

> *I have thought that if he does transition, he can always come live with me, and start fresh at a new school.* —Aunt of a gender-variant 7-year-old boy

Handling Negative Reactions

> *I know a few people who do not support us in this, and we have given them info on it and tried to explain it, to no avail. These are*

not your friends, so keep them away from your children. —Parent
of a 7-year-old transboy

There are different degrees of negative reaction to your child. When
someone starts to react in a visibly negative way it is best to stop them
before they get too far. Put your hand up and say something such as "I
was not actually asking for your opinion" or "Please do not speak neg-
atively in front of my child." If they persist in their negativity, you
should leave the situation. Do not flee. Do not yell. Rather, let them
know in no uncertain terms that this way of speaking about you, your
child, or your family is completely unacceptable, and therefore you are
leaving at once.

Someone may act outrageously in response to learning about your
child. They may wage a campaign to get your child out of the school, jeer
at you when your family arrives at the baseball field, try to prevent your
child from participating in camps, sports, and classes. You should simply go to the person in charge and describe the discrimination your child
is experiencing. They will most often switch your child to a different
team or class day.

If you or your child experience ongoing discrimination and you
have already addressed your concerns with the person in charge, you
may need to work your way up the chain of command in hopes of a
better resolution. For example, it may not be enough to simply talk to
a team coach, but a league manager or division manager instead. File
a formal complaint if the situation demands it. Keep a record of every
incident of harassment your child faces, and also every attempt you
make to rectify it. If you decide to pursue legal action, this evidence
will be helpful in proving your case. You may need to contact legal
assistance knowledgeable about civil rights or transgender rights
issues. See Chapter 9, Legal Issues to Consider, for resources. Discrimination of any kind is not acceptable, and you and your family do
not have to live with it.

Emotional Reactions of Adults and Older Children

It is essential to remember that *anxiety creates a primitive response in people*. Adults and some older children can feel misled and betrayed when they find out that someone they know is transgender or has a gender identity different from their presentation. It is helpful to remember that the only thing that has betrayed them is their own belief system. You and your child have done nothing wrong. No one's health or safety is at risk, no one has been lied to. The question of genitalia is different from the question of gender. It is culturally inappropriate to discuss what is in anyone's pants, and any assumption we make about what is in there is speculation. Nonetheless, many people still feel entitled to know this information. Be strong, hold on to your truth, and give people a chance to come around.

When Someone Finds Out By Accident

> *I fear what would happen if other kids see him. We work with a therapist on how to deal with this sort of thing—what our child can say if someone happens to see his privates, or remembers him as a girl from before.* —Parent of a 7-year-old transboy

If your child does not disclose to others that they are transgender, they always run the risk of someone finding out. If someone does find out by accident, remember that everyone involved has some responsibility for how the situation is handled. All parties have a choice in how they respond: you, your child, the person who found out. And if this happens in a social setting such as at school, or on a sports team, or at camp, the greater institution has a choice about how to respond.

As the parent, you have the role of guiding others in such a situation. Prepare a mental list of responses to have ready. It is advisable to obtain a letter from a doctor stating that your child is transgender, that this is a real condition you and your family live with, and that there is no deception or ill will involved. This can be helpful if someone calls Child Protective Services believing that you are engaging in child abuse. Also keep the name and number of several legal references handy in case you need to call someone—or threaten to. React calmly, and know your rights. If you need to leave a bad situation that has become unsafe for yourself or your child, do so. This enables you to retain your dignity and regroup before you have to deal further with the situation.

Preparing Your Child for Possible Adversity

Spending time helping your child develop coping mechanisms is an essential part of raising a gender-variant or transgender child. It is important to teach them resiliency in the face of adversity, and it is critical to help them develop a strong sense of self-esteem. This can be done in many ways, including therapy, martial arts training, and attending anti-bullying classes. Role-playing can be an incredibly valuable technique for working with your child to prepare for negative reactions. Once you are comfortable with your own responses to the range of possible negative reactions, you can start to model effective responses for your child. When you have explored worst-case scenarios together in advance and prepared a few possible responses, an actual negative reaction or undesired exposure becomes much less threatening. Remember that as your child grows and situations change, you will need to keep brainstorming new responses.

There are numerous books for parents about enhancing self-esteem in their children. Research these techniques and use them on a daily basis. Likewise, teach your child how to trust their instincts and intuition, and how to identify safe people when in a public setting. Teach them how to use their lungs to cry for help, and how to use age-appropriate self-defense techniques to protect themselves.

Allowing your child time to practice responses to teasing and ridicule can be enormously helpful. Explain that bullies go after vulnerable targets. If your child lets the taunting roll right off them, there is no point for the teasing to continue. A bully will go pick on someone they can get a rise out of.

Family Photos

One of the saddest times for a parent is when their transgender child asks them to remove pre-transition photos from display. This may feel like a move of finality, as if the baby and the young child you knew is really going away for good. It can be very painful.

Just remember that you can keep all of these photos in your own albums. You will still have the memories and visual reminders of the path your child has taken. Perhaps you can even keep a small picture on display in a private area, such as by your bedside. No one can take your memories or photos away from you. You are just showing respect for your child by not displaying them in a more public fashion. Do remember to be careful about showing family albums to anyone who does not know the full history of your child's gender.

Some families do not have to worry about this. If your child is open about being transgender, the photos can often remain on display.

We were going through some old pictures and we came across one of our son when he was 3 in a summer dress, and he showed our guest and said "See what a cute little girl I was?" which of course led to some explaining. —Parent of a 7-year-old transboy

But if your child selectively chooses whom to tell, they usually request the removal of any evidence that would do that disclosing for them.

Commonly Asked Questions and How to Answer Them

We end this chapter with some commonly asked questions you will likely encounter when first disclosing to others that your child is transgender. It may be especially helpful to memorize a few so you feel prepared and do not become defensive or embarrassed. Although much of this is discussed elsewhere in the book, we know that having these answers handy in one place will be helpful to many families.

Why is your child transgender?

No one really knows. But research is beginning to show that some people are just born that way.

Did you do something to cause this?

No one can make a child transgender, or change a child's gender identity. Its just part of who they are, like being left-handed.

Is there a cure?

Being transgender is not an illness. It is a gender identity. We all have a gender identity; in most people it matches their birth sex, but in some it does not. We want our child to be happy and healthy, and we know that this means allowing them to express their own gender identity.

Can't you make your child be normal?

Trying to make a child forget or suppress their true gender identity is nearly impossible, and studies show it is also hurtful. And I would appreciate it if you could see our child as normal.

Can't therapy or a doctor help?

We have seen a doctor who specializes in transgender children, and we have been told our child is happy and healthy the way they are.

Will he/she grow out of it?

Some children who are gender-variant decide to resume living as their birth sex, but most don't. We will support our child in either case.

Won't other kids tease him/her?

Probably this will happen, since all children are teased at some point about something. But our role as parents is to love and accept our child, and we will help them learn how to deal with teasing. We will do as much as we can to educate those around our child—in our family, our community, and our child's schools. Education increases understanding.

Will your child be able to go to a normal school?

Since there is nothing wrong with our child, they can go to any school. We hope that our school will accommodate and accept our child as it has learned to do with other children who are different. All schools are actually required to keep all their students safe. There is training to help schools become more sensitive to gender-variant and transgender students.

Will they have surgery? How is it done?

This is something we will have to discuss as a family when and if it becomes an issue. If you want to learn more about these issues, I can refer you to some websites.

Chapter 7

The Educational System and Your Family

OF ALL THE ISSUES parents face when raising a transgender or gender-variant child, the one they often struggle with most is how to work with their child's school. Parents wonder: Is it wise and safe to let my child attend school as their affirmed gender? Is it wise to allow them to transition during the school years? They wonder about how to inform and even educate the school about their child. They agonize over how to protect their child from teasing and bullying, and how to ensure that their child has a safe restroom to use. And they wonder, if their child plans to leave for college one day, how will they find a trans-friendly school and living environment?

Children spend the majority of their waking hours in school. Over the years they spend significantly more time with their classmates and teachers than they do with their parents. A child's experience at school can significantly enhance or undermine their sense of self. Furthermore, children need to feel emotionally safe in order to learn effectively. A welcoming and supportive school where bullying and teasing is not permitted and children are actively taught to respect and celebrate difference is the ideal environment for all children. This is especially true for gender-variant and transgender children, who frequently are the targets of teasing and bullying. A child cannot feel emotionally safe, and will most likely experience problems in learning, if they regularly experience discrimination at school. Nonetheless, even a school with a strong anti-bullying policy and anti-bias philosophy will still need training around gender-variant and transgender students.

> *Our biggest issue with the school was their lack of knowledge. At first it was suggested that we switch schools to one that is 12 miles away. Thanks. The problem is not the kids, it's the parents who call and say, "I don't want my kid in that class because they are teaching gay stuff." I find myself telling the teacher what to say to a child who knew my kid as a girl in kindergarten when she asks if she will change into a boy too. What to say to parents is hard and I tried to write out something that will suffice with the parents and the school to address the transgender issue. I gave it to the principal and we had a meeting with all the staff who may be in my kid's life. We covered the basics, like in choir please don't make my child sing with the girls. I am so glad that this fall he will be in school as a male. He is one of the guys and can use whatever restroom he wants.* —Parent of a 7-year-old transboy

Working with Your School

Each and every parent who has a significantly gender-variant or transgender student will have to work with their child's schools to ensure physical and emotional safety for their child. At the present, it is not standard practice for schools to receive training on the issues surrounding gender diversity. You must be proactive. Many parents assume that the teachers will do the necessary work to reduce the likelihood of bullying and teasing at school. This is not the case in most school environments. Unless you guide your teacher and let them know what your expectations are and how they can get training on the subject, despite their best intentions they will most likely be completely unaware of how to assist your child proactively. At Gender Spectrum, Stephanie and her staff spend the majority of their time educating schools—staff, teachers, parents, and students—about gender diversity.

If you wait until you hear from your child about problems at school, you have lost valuable time in assisting the staff to learn how to ensure the safety of your child. You are then playing catch-up with a force that would have been much easier to nip in the bud.

One reason we have written this book is to give parents a resource to share with their child's school principal, teachers, guidance counselor, and school nurse. Consider sharing this book with your PTA and local and district school boards. Bring the book to the diversity committee of your school. If there is none, consider starting one, or at least starting a gender equity committee.

Preschools and Pre-K Programs

Most preschools are privately run. They follow their own philosophies and are generally open to parental suggestions and involvement. As the children attending are still young, preschools tend to be more flexible about dress and play standards with regard to gender conformity. If a preschool proves a poor fit, parents usually have the option to take their child, and their dollars, elsewhere.

Many pre-K programs are run in public school facilities and, as such, are bound to follow rules and guidelines that the general school population must abide by.

Kindergarten

In some regions a family gets to choose what kindergarten their child will attend. In others there is only one school, or there is a lottery. Some schools may be known as more accepting of diversity, depending on a mixture of geographic location, parental involvement, state laws, and the leadership of the principals and area superintendents. Parents may get the school they are hoping for, but sometimes they may not. In either case, there is usually not much knowledge about transgender children in most school districts. Parents will therefore have to be ready to advocate for their children.

Getting any child and family ready for kindergarten involves both excitement and stress. For families with gender-variant and transgender children, there are additional issues to contend with, including fears for a child's emotional and possibly physical safety.

We recommend that every family with a gender-variant or transgender student entering kindergarten speak directly with the principal prior to the start of the school year. This is best not left until the last minute. Introducing yourself and your situation ahead of time allows the school to do the necessary work to ensure the safety and support of your child.

It is also appropriate to request a meeting with your student's teacher prior to the beginning of the school year. Even if it is the policy of the school not to announce the child's teacher until the school year begins, the principal will often make an exception when there are special needs that must be addressed from the very first day.

If you cannot know which teacher will be assigned to your child, try to meet with all of the possible teachers before school starts. This allows them time to integrate your situation and to ask you relevant questions about your child. It also allows them time to do the necessary personal work required if they have beliefs that would interfere with the natural support of your child. In this way, the principal can assign your child to the teacher most capable of and excited about working with your child.

Personal beliefs or philosophies should not factor into public education. All children have the right to learn in a safe environment, free of bullying. To ensure this security for a gender-variant child, the teacher has to be proactive and set the tone for the entire class, and both for the students and their parents.

Should Other Families Be Informed?

Information about students is private unless you wish others to be informed of it. For example, no administrator or teacher is allowed to share personal information about your child with other parents. It is confidential. However, if you wish to inform your child's class that your child is gender-variant or transgender, you may do so. The teacher can then follow your lead in how you want to handle this.

Some families have found it helpful, with the support of the school, to send a letter to parents with some basic information about their child, either before the start of classes or during the first week of school. This can be especially helpful, for example, if the child attended the same school the past year as the opposite gender and you and the school administration perceive the parent body as a welcoming community. Some parents have chosen to write this sort of letter when their child starts kindergarten. The training staff at Gender Spectrum feel this may work best with children in the lower grades and with children of all ages in small private schools. They also advise parents to "be prepared for the backlash." The possibility of backlash should be discussed with the school administration in advance, so that they are not left wondering what to do if another parent complains publicly or states that "they are teaching gay stuff" in your child's classroom or requests that their child be transferred to a different class.

If you choose to write a letter, it should be unapologetic in tone, explanatory in a rudimentary way, and short, and it should make clear this is just one factor about your child along with commonalities such as loving puppies, the color green, and spaghetti. It should also state in a positive way that you expect support and kindness for your child. Emphasize as well that you're aware other parents may have questions— and that these can be addressed in an appropriate venue if necessary. Some parents have encouraged their schools to keep "community books" in each classroom, to which every child or family contributes a short personal description. This takes the onus off a particular family for being "different" and lets everyone share what is special and unique about themselves.

The letter approach may work best in more liberal areas or where your family is not alone in blazing a trail of gender diversity. The risks and benefits must be carefully weighed. Some schools feel that such a letter would incite negative reactions from families and place all of the focus on your child, whereas other schools feel it increases the support and understanding of the parent body.

Indeed, the letter approach is not for everyone. We recommend it only when the child's parents are in agreement about this approach, there is strong school support, and preparation has been made for any possible backlash. There should also be an ongoing gender sensitivity training program in place in the school. As one parent remarked, "This is part of an ongoing process for the school as a whole, it is not just about jumping through hoops for our one child. Yes, the school may have realized the need for such work because of our child, but they are committed to teaching gender diversity to everyone in the school." Another said, "We initially thought we would send a letter. We thought that would prevent teasing of our child. But then after working with the principal we realized that it would be better to hold a staff training about gender variance and then a parent education night about gender variance instead. This way the education happens but the reactions are not directed as much toward my child, but more toward the administrations for their accepting policies. We are greatly relieved we approached it that way." We realize that parents are forging new ground here, and we recommend connecting with other parents who have dealt with this issue successfully in their child's school for further ideas.

Private or Public School?

For some families, there is a choice to make between public and private schools. The family finances may allow for private school, or financial aid is available, or perhaps lower-cost private schooling is available, such as subsidized religious education.

There are two main advantages for transgender kids in many progressive private schools: the school's philosophy may be inclusive of gender variance, or at least open to it, and because class size is smaller and teachers often more motivated, there may be more opportunity to teach understanding and respect for differences. Certainly many public schools also set a high bar for tolerance, but private schools may actually seek out diverse families and children and work closely with them to guarantee that their experience is a good one. This may also result in more comprehensive staff training.

In addition, parents may be able to influence school policies better in private schools, where the parent body is smaller and more involved. Indeed, some private schools, such as the Bay Area's Park Day School and Aurora School, are on the cutting edge of gender sensitivity and transgender inclusiveness. While the Bay Area is more progressive on many matters than elsewhere in the country, progressive philosophies will eventually spread to other regions of the country, especially if parents are advocating for these changes. However, as with other issues of bias, a school's willingness to work openly on gender issues is affected by religious affiliation, school philosophy, and geographic location—not to mention the personal beliefs of the school administration, teachers, and staff.

Homeschooling Options

More and more families of all backgrounds are choosing to school their children at home. Some families with gender-variant or transgender children are making this choice as well. Perhaps this might be your educational method of choice. But if you are considering homeschooling as an option to shelter your child from harassment for their gender variance, the choice to homeschool must be balanced with your child's ability to learn to walk in the world, secure in their gender expression and gender identity. Families who choose to homeschool their gender-variant young children must also work hard not to make their child feel that there is something wrong or shameful about them. In other words, be clear about your motivations and what they communicate to your child. It is not a good idea to hide your child from the world and in so doing to teach your child to feel shame. As parents, it is essential to teach your gender-variant child coping skills and pride, whether they attend school at home with you or with others in a traditional school setting.

On the other hand, some families choose to homeschool after working with their child's school to no avail, especially if their child has been the subject of undue teasing or violence and their child's mental, physical, or emotional safety is at risk. If you decide to press legal charges, or bring in social advocates for your child, please know that it is a lengthy process to change a system unwilling to address its gender discrimination. So, for the safety of your child, you may choose to school at home while things settle down, or until you locate another school.

A common time to commence homeschooling is when a teen emerges as transgender and does not want to transition at school. The teen may take a year or part of a year off while starting physical transition such as hormones and learning to live full-time as the other gender. When a child is afforded this option, it can significantly reduce the stress they face in making such radical external and internal changes under public scrutiny. These children sometimes return to the same school in their new identity, while others begin the next year at a new school.

When Your Child Has Other Special Needs

Being gender-variant or transgender is only one aspect of your child. If your child has additional qualities that put them at greater risk for bias and therefore teasing or discrimination, their gender identity or expression can compound and confuse the situation.

My transgender child has a speech impediment. Somehow this combination of less common characteristics positions him as the target of unending teasing. It seems like the teacher does not intervene as much as she would for other children. It's like there is an unspoken attitude that he's inviting teasing by having two special needs. As if he could choose! —Parent of an 8-year-old genderfluid boy

My son has been to three different schools and he's only in second grade. There are no other schools in our district left for him to go to, and we can't afford private school. He has "behavioral issues." I can't get them to see that allowing him to be tormented every day because of what he wears and how he acts creates a need for him to defend himself and fight back. What else is he supposed to do if the teachers don't stick up for him? Their response to me is always the same, "If he's suffering because he wears girls' clothes and acts like a girl, don't send him to school in those clothes. It's up to you to change his appearance so that he will fit in at school." I always ask them, "If I said he was being teased and bullied because of the color of his skin, would you ask me to paint him?" Give me a break! But we cannot find a school that will stick up for him. We can't tell him to change. We've tried it, he wouldn't leave his room. He asked us to kill him so he could go to heaven where God understands him. —Parent of a 7-year-old gender-variant son

Work diligently with your school to ensure that your child's special needs are met.

If Your Child Is Experiencing Harassment or Discrimination at School

If your child is facing discrimination at school, you do not have to tolerate it. Take action. There are legal options as well as training organizations

Are LGBT students at risk of experiencing harassment and discrimination in schools?

Yes. There is now extensive evidence that LGBT students are disproportionately targeted for harassment and discrimination in schools. Left unchecked, this harassment and discrimination may often escalate to the level of physical violence or violent crime.

Specifically, results from the 2001 National School Climate Survey indicate that:

- Over 80 percent of LGBT students reported being verbally harassed because of their sexual orientation; and
- Nearly 70 percent of LGBT students reported feeling unsafe in school because of their sexual orientation.

Moreover, studies also indicate that school officials often fail to respond to or, in some cases, even participate in, the discrimination and harassment. One study documented this problem, reporting that:

- 80 percent of prospective teachers reported negative attitudes toward LGBT people; and
- 66 percent of guidance counselors maintain negative feelings about and toward LGBT people.

[Source: National Center for Lesbian Rights website. Used with permission.]

established to address the complaints you file. School districts can be held liable under existing federal law for failing to protect students from harassment based on sexual orientation and gender nonconformity. Make sure your school is aware that you know your legal rights and will exercise them. If they do not protect your child—take action.

How schools can support gender-variant and transgender children: A step-by-step guide

There are a number of relatively simple things that each school can do to dramatically increase the comfort and safety of gender-variant and transgender students. It takes a commitment on the part of the school to implement these changes. Some of these changes are administrative tasks that can be performed by volunteer parents. Others require more of a system overhaul.

1. Create a Supportive Organizational School Culture

Creating an inclusive school culture requires a comprehensive approach based on defining core values and consistently reinforcing them. Although nondiscrimination policies are the cornerstone of organizational change, schools cannot achieve inclusiveness by simply adopting policies. A school must authentically understand and convey the value of inclusiveness and reinforce this message at all levels. Every student, teacher, administrator, coach, bus driver, parent, and member of support staff (before and after school), security, food service, and custodial staff involved in the school should know and understand the school's commitment to treating every person with respect, valuing and affirming differences, and confronting harassment and discrimination of any kind. It all boils down to every person being equally deserving of kindness and respect.

2. Adopt Zero Tolerance for Discrimination

Schools can make a very powerful statement by including gender expression and gender identity in the official school nondiscrimination policy. Written policies that prohibit discrimination based on perceived sexual orientation and gender identity and presentation make it clear that discrimination and harassment will not be tolerated. The existence of such a policy also gives staff the support they need to respond appropriately to such discrimination and to actively implement the school's values in the classroom.

It is important to note that such a policy does not infringe on individual beliefs about gender roles or sexual orientation. Members of the school community are free to hold any beliefs they choose, so long as they enforce and adhere to the school's nondiscrimination policy.

Schools can ensure that all teachers, families, staff, and students are aware of the school's nondiscrimination policy by:

- Including a copy of the policy in the staff training and orientation for every new employee, contractor, and teacher. This includes specialists, substitutes, bus drivers, and before- and after-school staff.
- Discussing the implementation of the policy to help all employees understand what it means to provide safety to gender-variant and transgender students.
- Including the policy in all written handbook or orientation materials provided to each family in the school.
- Discussing the policy each school year with every child as part of the curriculum and introduction to the school year.
- Posting the policy in strategic locations around the school.

3. Update Policies and Forms

A simple but important administrative task is to update all written policies and forms to reflect gender-inclusive language. This includes application forms, surveys, questionnaires, and the like. When presented with more than two options under the category of gender, families and students are provided the opportunity to accurately reflect their genders. Making these small but significant changes to school forms also communicates to everyone an acceptance of gender variance.

For example, on a form that asks for gender, instead of providing only the standard male/female choices, the form could read this way:

Please check the boxes that apply to you.

Sex/Gender Identity:

Male

Female

Transgender

Please tell us if you have other words to express your gender.

Comments:

If any of this information is confidential, please be sure to designate it here.

4. Honor Preferred Names and Pronouns

It is the responsibility of the school to honor all students' preferred names and pronouns. Many transgender students do not use their legal names. School forms should include the question "What name do you prefer to be called?" The school must enter this name into the database so that it shows up on attendance rolls. This will prevent daily discomfort or outing when a child is called by their legal name. For report cards, it is usually necessary to use the legal name, but the preferred name can be used as well. For example, "David, legal name Karen Black." The same is true for pronoun use. Honor the pronoun that the student prefers to goes by. When in doubt, ask. Pronoun choice is not up to the school or the teacher; it is determined by the student and is based on their asserted gender identity.

5. Develop Guidelines for Transgender Students

With the help of gender educators, your school can develop written

policies pertaining to transgender students and areas of potential problems. For example, the school should establish policies regarding
school identification cards, locker room policies, athletic clubs, athletic teams, camping trips, sex-segregated classes or activities, bathrooms, legal name changes, maintaining privacy about transgender
status when desired, and requests for past transcripts after legal
name changes.

We reprint here a few sections of the policies of the State of California and the San Francisco Unified School District pertaining to gender discrimination. You can find the entire documentation online.

California Law Prohibits Gender-Based Discrimination in Public Schools

The California Education Code states that "all pupils have
the right to participate fully in the educational process, free
from discrimination and harassment." Cal. Ed. Code Section 201(a). Section 220 of the Education Code provides
that no person shall be subject to discrimination on the
basis of gender in any program or activity conducted by an
educational institution that receives or benefits from state
financial assistance.

The California Code of Regulations defines "gender" as:
"a person's actual sex or perceived sex and includes a person's perceived identity, appearance, or behavior, whether
or not that identity, appearance, or behavior is different from
that traditionally associated with a person's sex at birth." 5
CCR Section 4910(k).

SFUSD Board Policy Prohibits Gender-Based Harassment

Names/Pronouns Students shall have the right to be
addressed by a name and pronoun corresponding to their
gender identity that is exclusively and consistently asserted at

school. Students are not required to obtain a court ordered name and/or gender change or to change their official records as a prerequisite to being addressed by the name and pronoun that corresponds to their gender identity.

Official Records The District shall change a student's official records to reflect a change in legal name or gender upon receipt of documentation that such legal name and/or gender have been changed pursuant to California legal requirements.

Restroom Accessibility Students shall have access to the restroom that corresponds to their gender identity exclusively and consistently asserted at school. Where available, a single stall bathroom may be used by any student who desires increased privacy, regardless of the underlying reason. The use of such a single stall bathroom shall be a matter of choice for a student, and no student shall be compelled to use such bathroom.

Locker Room Accessibility Transgender students shall not be forced to use the locker room corresponding to their gender assigned at birth.

Sports and Gym Class Transgender students shall not be denied the opportunity to participate in physical education, nor shall they be forced to have physical education outside of the assigned class time. Generally, students should be permitted to participate in gender-segregated recreational gym class activities and sports in accordance with the student's gender identity that is exclusively and consistently asserted at school.

Dress Codes Students shall have the right to dress in accordance with their gender identity that is exclusively and consistently asserted at school, within the constraints of the dress codes adopted at their school site.

The Option of Special Education

Because of state laws concerning equal opportunity and protection, gender-variant children may qualify for participation in special education classes in many school districts. This is an option some parents are exploring to allow their children to attend public school in a more protected environment. Consult the policies of your own state or province for further ideas about special education.

6. Provide Staff Training

Because of the lack of general understanding of the nuances of gender diversity and how to keep gender-variant children safe at school, it is essential for any school with gender-variant or transgender students to provide training to members of their staff. To effectively counter discrimination, the school must provide both initial and ongoing training to all school personnel. Education and training is a crucial part of creating cultural change. It reinforces the school's commitment to an inclusive environment and replaces common myths and misconceptions with practical, evidence-based information regarding gender vari-

A 2007 report called "the GENIUS Index" (Gender Equality National Index for Universities and Schools) analyzed data on inclusive policies for K–12 schools and universities, including gender identity/expression. It found that "more than 100 public K–12 school districts, encompassing thousands of individual schools, have extended these new protections to nearly 3.5 million children in 24 states." This includes both large urban areas and small rural systems. States with the largest concentration of districts include California, Iowa, New Jersey, New York, and Wisconsin. The report is available from the Gender Public Advocacy Coalition (GenderPAC) website: www.gpac.org/genius/2007.pdf.

ance in children. Additionally, as staff and students change, new members of the community must be educated. It is not enough to establish a schoolwide policy; the school must provide the tools and support to make this commitment a reality.

Professional training is an integral resource for implementing a schoolwide gender nondiscrimination policy. All teachers and staff members should fully understand the gender policy to respond effectively to questions from families about what the policy means. The training program should include specific ideas for creating safety and support for gender expression in the classroom, as well as ongoing support for teachers.

A strong training curriculum covers the following topics:

- An explanation of pertinent vocabulary and definitions
- Developmental issues and adaptive strategies for supporting gender-variant and transgender children and teens
- Tools to promote the positive development of gender-variant and transgender children and teens
- A review of what an emerging awareness of gender identity in children may look like and how families and schools can support a child through this process
- A discussion of how gender identity and sexual orientation may or may not be linked
- Identification of the issues and challenges unique to gender-variant and transgender students
- Community resources available to serve gender-variant and transgender children, teens, and their families, as well as their allies
- Identifying warning signs that indicate at-risk students and families

The teacher trainings should include curricular concerns and developmentally appropriate language that teachers can use in their classrooms and on the playground.

Trainers can engage all participants in open discussions that encourage them to ask questions. The trainings should emphasize practical solutions and provide concrete suggestions for creating gender-affirming environments. These suggestions may include:

- Adopting and enforcing a policy prohibiting slurs or jokes based on race, culture, gender, gender identity, sexual orientation or any other typology
- Displaying posters or symbols that indicate an inclusive environment
- Providing school libraries with books, magazines, and videos with gender-fluid and gender-nonconforming characters and themes
- Using respectful and inclusive terminology that avoids making assumptions about any individual's gender identity
- Creating opportunities for dialogue with students and staff about these issues
- Modeling age-appropriate language
- Incorporating gender-aware language and curriculum in the classroom and developing skills to address issues that arise with gender-variant and transgender students

When we heard that Matthew was transgender we couldn't believe it. He had attended our K–12 school from the start. And now, as a junior we find out he's really a girl and has felt that way for more than 10 years. This has been a turning point for me in my 20-year career as a teacher. I taught him throughout middle school and did not have a clue. I am so glad we received this training. I now realize that I cannot make assumptions about my students. Not only that, but I need to actively create a safe space so that my students realize that it is OK to be themselves.
—Middle-school science teacher

I walked up to Carter and asked how his older brother was. He looked at me like I was a monster. He literally turned and ran. It was only later that I understood what had happened. I didn't know that his brother was now his sister. He clearly did not know what to say and needed to escape. I'm so glad that our school has now received some training on all of this. I had no idea how much there is to learn and what a burden it can be for all family members to live in a society that simply is ignorant about transgender issues. I certainly didn't mean to traumatize Carter. It was an innocent question—but one he must live in fear of on a daily basis. —Elementary-school teacher

7. Provide Parent Education

Some schools find that it is beneficial to communicate their gender policy to the entire parent community in a form other than school handouts. The following is a sample schoolwide communication about gender for use by any elementary school.

At our school we support the variance of gender expression that children show us is possible. We understand and uphold that gender is a spectrum that includes many variations between what is traditionally acknowledged as male and female. For some adults this possibility may be new or confusing. However, for children it is easy.

For some, gender is fluid: "Sometimes I feel like a boy, and sometimes I feel like a girl." For others, gender identity is incongruous with one's anatomical sex—"I feel like a boy in a girl's body," or vice versa. Still others proclaim that their gender is neither male nor female, while some feel that they are both. Rather than dismissing or correcting such statements as nonsense, we acknowledge and affirm that self-knowledge and the freedom to express oneself fully is integral to the development of self-esteem.

At our school we recognize that every human has the right to decide who they are—it is not within anyone else's power to decide for another who they are. Because of our school's philosophy, you may hear things at home such as "I assume that person is a male—but I can't really know unless I ask them" or "Most boys have penises, but not all." Although anatomical terms may enter conversations about gender, there is no discussion of sexuality in our elementary school curriculum. You may also hear references to bigender, a boy in a girl's body, transgender, or typical boy or typical girl. If you have any questions about these terms please feel free to ask your child and to come to us for greater explanation.

Some schools have found it helpful to address the parent body directly every year in an evening presentation about gender diversity. The educational components for parents are most effective if they provide foundational information about gender identity development and children as well as provide ample opportunity to answer questions. In Stephanie's experience at Gender Spectrum, she has learned that these evenings can be very tense for some parents. As a result, we recommend that parent education events be facilitated by highly experienced professionals who can reassure the concerned parents and speak with ease to the age appropriateness of the subject. Gender Spectrum trainings combine informative and inspirational lectures and videos with a panel of gender-diverse individuals and parents of gender-variant children to make the subject accessible and real to the parents.

Parent trainings should include a review of the school's gender policy and a component on how to address potential discrepancies between personal beliefs and school policy. It is very helpful to spend time on terms and definitions. It is also valuable to dispel existing myths and stereotypes surrounding transgender people. The goal of parent education evenings is to adopt a common understanding of the following facts and principles:

- Anatomy and gender are not interchangeable.
- Some babies are born with ambiguous genitalia, as in various intersex conditions.
- Gender identity is a subjective sense of self.
- Gender-variant children are a minority group that deserves protection.
- There are more than two expressions of core gender identity, such as feeling you are nongendered, or have a blended gender.

8. Provide Student Education

Students also need gender education. Any school with a gender discrimination policy must educate students about what it means and why it is important. This is a rich opportunity for the student body to receive education in gender diversity. Often these presentations are cosponsored by the school's gay–straight alliance, which arranges for a speaker or panel to address a school assembly about gender diversity and respect. This is an opportunity to remind the student body of the consequences of breaking the school policy.

Stephanie's school events with Gender Spectrum begin with an assembly and then break into smaller groups throughout the day for more intimate discussion and questions. This format allows students to grasp a deeper understanding of what gender diversity means and how it already affects them. These trainings also provide students with tools for recognizing harassment based on gender and language and sticking up for transgender and gender-variant students.

I really didn't understand what was going on for Mike. One day he was Mike and then the next day he told us he was really a girl and wanted to be called Mikki. When they came and spoke to us, I really got it! I hadn't wanted to ask Mikki all sorts of personal questions and yet I couldn't stop thinking about them. The presentation really let me see her as a girl and forget about the other parts that seemed so weird at first. —Peer of a trans high school student

Educating all students, regardless of their age, is very important when a child is transitioning at the school. For a child to be accepted, they need to be understood. Age-appropriate lesson plans on gender diversity for elementary classrooms are easily prepared. Gender Spectrum works with elementary schools to provide in-class time with students and support for teachers in creating a gender-respectful classroom. A key component for increasing the safety of gender-nonconforming students is to adopt a strong anti-teasing policy, a strong self-esteem curriculum, and a strong ally-building curriculum.

We were very nervous about allowing the student to come to school as a girl. But we realized that we needed to do the right thing. How can we say we value diversity and we respect one another and then pick and choose whom that applies to? —Head of a private parochial school

Park Day School in Oakland, California, which has received this training from Gender Spectrum, has published a policy paper about the school's process and self-awareness on these issues. The paper, written by Susan Lee, is entitled "When It Counts: Talking about Transgender Identity and Gender Fluidity in Elementary School." It is available online at the Gender Spectrum Family website, www.genderspectrum.org (click on "Family Conference" for more information). The paper will prove to be an informative and inspirational starting point for other schools and families who want to better understand how to incorporate inclusiveness and gender awareness into their school's curriculum and policies. Here is an excerpt from that document:

As responsible educators, we cannot ignore that in recent years the taboo around discussing transgender identity has opened up. From Oprah to Tyra Banks to newsmagazines covering transgender issues, the topic is surfacing now more than ever. Teaching children that every human should be allowed equal rights and the power to self-identify is a necessary responsibility that educators must take on. When these discussions are allowed to happen, we celebrate the accomplishments of both the person and the society that allows for human differences. At the end of each day, we cannot help but be proud that as an institution, we have taken steps forward by sticking to our gut instincts and respecting the needs of all children to feel safe at school. Talking about issues of transgender identity will not magically turn all children toward identifying as transgender, nor will it "confuse" children when discussions are led with intentionality and explicitness. Informing our students is the best thing we can do so that they are empowered to act as responsive and courageous citizens.

9. Ensure Bathroom Safety for All Students

All children need to have their basic physical needs met. This includes having a right to go to the bathroom safely. Gender-variant children and teens usually do not feel comfortable in the binary bathroom system. Children as young as 3 admit to holding their pee to the point of wetting their pants in order to avoid this stress. Younger children can feel confused about which bathroom to use, and just having to choose a bathroom is too much stress for some gender-variant children. If they choose the bathroom they feel they belong in, others are made uncomfortable, but choosing the other bathroom makes *them* uncomfortable— it feels like a no-win situation. Gender-variant and transgender children and teens are subjected to teasing, ridicule, and sometimes violence if they are perceived to be in the wrong bathroom.

Schools can handle this problem directly and easily by providing single-occupant bathrooms, and where there are gender-specific bathrooms, providing privacy in the stalls. Some bathrooms can be desig-nated as unisex or gender-neutral.

It is important that these private or gender-neutral bathrooms be made available to all children, not just the one child who has self-identified as gender-variant or as transgender. Even if unisex bathrooms are provided, some transgender students may choose to use the bathroom designated for their gender. Each person should be allowed to use the bathroom of their consistently asserted gender.

10. Document Harassment of Gender-variant Students

Guidelines for documenting and addressing harassment based on gen-der discrimination need to be established. In the event of harassment, it is essential that a school respond quickly and visibly to set clear stan-dards indicating a zero tolerance for acts of violence or harassment. Where it is relevant, school security guards and safety personnel need to be trained in these policies as well.

To evaluate the implementation and performance of nondiscrimina-tion policies, the school should keep written records of each complaint and its resolution. It is also helpful to designate an overseeing body or individual to review the grievance records regularly to identify potential problems, patterns, or the need for additional training.

11. Provide Resources and Support for Families with Gender-variant Children

It is a sign of the times that children are becoming aware of their gen-der identity at increasingly younger ages—families are confronting issues of gender nonconformity while their children are in preschool, elementary school, middle school, and high school. Parents struggle to adapt to their child's gender variance or nonconformity. They are in urgent need of information, guidance, and contact with other families experiencing similar issues.

The availability of supportive resources and referrals within your school community may be the crucial piece in improving a child's self-esteem and mental health outcomes. Direct overtures should be made to families with gender-variant and transgender children. In fact, access to information and support may prevent or minimize family conflict or crisis by helping families understand what is happening. Families in crisis are more receptive to change because of their immediate need to relieve conflict and restore family harmony. Resources for families may save lives. Family rejection places a gender-variant child at risk. Information, education, and support are necessary to increase family communication and understanding, decrease family rejection, and preserve family relationships.

An easily accessible resource guide can be created by gathering and regularly updating materials and placing them in a binder for parents, staff, and students. The resource guide should include information not only about gender diversity, but also about local therapists and doctors who are known to be supportive. It should list updated Internet resources for families and for teens, including resources in the various languages spoken by the families in your community.

12. Conduct a Gender Sensitivity Inventory of Your School

The same overseeing individual or body that reviews the grievance records can conduct periodic inventories to make sure the school is gender-inclusive and transgender-sensitive and that the nondiscrimination policy is implemented with respect to gender diversity. This committee can be made up of parents or staff, or it can be a function of the school's diversity committee. The committee works to ensure that the school is a safe environment for gender-nonconforming students by:

- Encouraging gender-diverse role models through peer mentoring programs
- Establishing student, staff, and parent discussions addressing gender diversity

- Arranging for speakers from transgender organizations to speak to the student body
- Making sure there is at least one on-site staff person who can speak easily to the implementation of the diversity policy
- Encouraging all clubs to be gender-inclusive
- Maintaining the gender resource guide for staff, students, and families
- Evaluating curricula for gender-inclusive units and language

Addressing Gender in the Classroom

My son's teacher told us that she once needed to have an activity with two groups in the classroom, and she said to line up with boys on one side and girls on the other side. She told us our son went walking to the girls' group and they sent him back to the boy's group with a long face. —Parent of a 5-year-old gender-variant child

All the assumptions of school-age kids are so hard for my child— that pink is for girls, blue for boys, etc. —Parent of a 6-year-old gender-variant boy

Right now the biggest issue for Stevie is that most children play with traditional toys according to their sex. The biggest issue when Stevie gets older will be the possibility of trans- and homophobia arising from children who hear their parents talking. —Aunt of the same 6-year-old boy

For teachers to feel comfortable addressing the gender spectrum in the classroom, teacher training and the express support of the administration are usually required. As with all anti-bias issues, teachers feel greater ease addressing "hot" issues with the support of the school. Thus, as discussed, the first step is to start with a schoolwide policy. Then each teacher can create a supportive class policy and begin to implement ideas in the curriculum.

School provides a unique opportunity for children to learn to embrace their own gender and the genders expressed by others. Schools are uniquely poised to open the minds of students of all ages about gender diversity. Instead of reinforcing the accepted cultural training of gender, schools can teach children to think for themselves about gender. But how do teachers create such opportunities in the classroom, and what do teachers do when a gender-variant child is in the classroom?

The first step is to provide teacher training and materials so teachers can incorporate gender-aware language and curriculum. From there, the options are limitless:

- Use gender-neutral language as much as possible. This usually creates awkwardness at first, saying "children" instead of "boys and girls"; "What is that person doing?" instead of "What is that woman doing?"; "That belongs to Catherine" rather than to "him" or "her." With practice, using gender-neutral language becomes less awkward. Take care not to specify the gender of animals, as well.

- Be an ally and an advocate for gender-variant and transgender students. Teachers can strive to create a culture and an atmosphere where everyone is validated for being who they are. It is important to initiate discussions of gender variance; in their absence, a gender-variant or transgender student is likely to feel invisible and invalidated. However, you should try to conduct such a discussion without singling out any student—you want them to feel validated, not put on the spot.

- Challenge put-downs, and dispel myths and stereotypes. Be prepared to intervene. If actions or statements that are stereotypical, demeaning, ridiculing, or discriminating occur in your presence—step in and speak up. Demonstrate what it means to stand up for gender diversity.

- Respect the privacy of your students. Follow their lead. If you are ever in doubt about a student's gender, clarify it with them in private. Remember that it is a student's prerogative not to disclose their transgender status to you or the class.

- Include reflections of gender diversity in the curricula through films, articles, books, classroom posters, and guest speakers.

- Initiate discussion about how the way a person feels on the inside may differ from how they look on the outside. Encourage the children to think of objects or situations that look one way on the outside and another way on the inside—like a coconut. This helps lay the groundwork for further conversations about gender identity.

- Initiate discussions that encourage ally building. Bring up subjects where children in the class may need support and brainstorm how to support them. Eventually, bring up a hypothetical situation of a child who feels they are both a boy and a girl: how could each student act as an ally to that child? Or to a boy who wears skirts to school?

- If it is age-appropriate, explore with the students how it would be to hear that someone in the class did not have the expected anatomy that reflects their gender. Does this make the person any different from how they have always been? Bring this exercise back to ally building.

- Give the students an exercise in which they have to speak and write all day or all week long without using any gender-specific language.

- Show books and images that reflect people wearing dress or hairstyles atypical for their gender, engaged in activities atypical for their gender, and likewise images of people with ambiguous gender expression.

- Ask the class to create new pronouns and language to use in speech and writing. Examples of current usage in the transgender community are nongendered pronouns such as hir, s/he, and ze.

- Refrain from separating groups by boys and girls. Find other ways to sort the class if needed.

- Ask the students to express in a journal how they know they are a boy or a girl. Do they ever feel that they are some of each? How would they know if no one told them whether they are a girl or a boy? If they didn't have to choose—would they? This is great fertile ground for sowing the idea that not all people feel their gender to be aligned with their anatomical sex.

- Explore with the students how it would feel to find out that their best friend really felt like a "boy" or a "girl" or a "heshe" even though they always thought them to be something else.

- Create a lesson plan called "In the classroom we support gender variance by…" and put it up on the wall.

When Your Child Is the Brunt of Other Parents' Fears

Other parents can be very afraid of transgender children if they haven't had any education in gender variance. Their anxiety about the unknown can cause them to act in a primal way. This commonly manifests as demanding that the transgender child not use the bathroom of their affirmed gender, forbidding play dates, and even insisting that their own child publicly shun the transgender child. Some parents ask for their child to be transferred to another class, and some even choose to remove their child from the school. In some instances, parents have created a smear campaign against the child's family by talking to as many parents and community members as possible in an inflammatory manner.

If this sort of reaction happens in your school community, you must call on the support of your administration. Here is where it helps to have an established policy on gender discrimination. It is also easy to see why it is important to have discussed your child's special needs and your family's expectations of the school *prior* to the beginning of the school year.

If it seems overwhelming to you or the staff to know what to do in this situation, it can be helpful to make an analogy with racial discrimination. Imagine these parents having the same reaction to a Hispanic child in the classroom: trying to make them use their own bathroom, refusing to have the child over to their home, refusing to let their child associate with the Hispanic child. Would you know what to do? Discrimination is bigotry any way you look at it.

Supporting Your Student

Throughout the years the needs of your child will change and evolve. For most parents of gender-variant and transgender students, the greatest work with the school is required in the beginning, whenever your child attends a new school, or if your child goes through a gender transition. However, there will be unexpected times when you need to take an active role once again with your child's school. Resist the assumption that if you spoke to the teacher last year and the staff was given some training you do not need to speak to your child's teacher this year, or next. You must communicate with your child's teachers every year. Remind the principal to select next year's teacher with your child's special situation in mind. Every time new specialists arrive at your child's school, such as gym or music teachers, you will need to discuss with them the particulars of your child and what you expect from them as a teacher.

If you have another child in the same school, it is important to ensure that this sibling is supported, as well. Make sure your school provides training to all teachers, parents, and students that each of your children will be exposed to. At first, parents may not feel that this is important, but many families realize the value of supporting each child in the family right from the start.

It wasn't my transgender child that was teased, it was actually her younger sister who struggled. She was teased mercilessly. Her teacher did not have any training and the school refused to pay for the training because our older child was at the middle school and this was the elementary school. Finally we hired a private trainer to talk with her. The results were remarkable. We just regret that we did not think to have arranged this right from the start. Of course, word would spread, other children have older siblings, too. —Parent of a 13-year-old trans son and a 10-year-old gender-typical daughter

Having a gender-variant or transgender child requires you, as their parent, to become their advocate. Even if you are shy and unassuming, you must overcome your own fears in support of your child. The time and energy it requires on your part will be well worth it—it may make the difference between their life and death. Supportive school and family experiences can help gender-variant and transgender teens develop the self-confidence and resilience necessary to form integrated, positive, and healthy identities.

Off to College: Choices and Challenges

While we realize that college may not be for everyone, nor is every college affordable for every transgender child and their family, it remains a rite of passage for many young people. You may have concerns and questions about what it will be like for your child once they leave home. It can be a relief to imagine a world beyond high school for your child. Where high school tends to be insular, college is a chance to expand beyond the familiar, to break away from regions and attitudes that may be oppressive for a young transgender person. Whether or not your child has begun any kind of physical transition, in college they will be offered the opportunity for transformation in several important and empowering ways. Leaving more prejudiced geographic areas, unsupportive peers, and even family trauma is incredibly freeing for transgender or gender-variant teens, as it often is for typically gendered young people, too.

Academia often leads the rest of society in accommodating transgender youth. This section examines the many issues involved with finding the most transgender-friendly environment for launching your child into independence.

Suggestions for College-Bound Transgender Students
- Develop a close circle of friends who support your transgender, genderqueer, or gender-variant identity.
- Find transgender-supportive faculty, staff, or administrators through college deans, LGBT student groups, and queer study programs.
- Look for a transgender group on campus; if there isn't one, see if there is an inclusive LGBTQ group.
- Find community resources for transgender folk in the area where you will be attending school. PFLAG chapters may also be a good source of information and support.
- Reach out to transgender students on other campuses—the Internet can help locate them.
- Join applicable email lists.

Finding a Transgender-Friendly College
Transgender high schoolers and their parents who are exploring college options no longer need to feel alone in this search. The Internet has made accessing this kind of information increasingly easier. Keep in mind that new sites will have appeared by the time this book is published, but the information below will get you started.

Your first stop for information online should be the Campus Climate Index, sponsored by the organization Campus Pride, a group specifically working to make the college years better for LGBTQ people. This site is also endorsed by the Consortium of Higher Education LGBTQ Resource

Professionals. The index enables students and their parents to find detailed information about the policies and practices of schools across the country. More information is at http://www.campusclimateindex.org. Transgender students can also find a wealth of information at the Transgender Law and Policy Institute, http://www.transgenderlaw.org/, which has specific sections for college students, including up-to-date lists of colleges with nondiscrimination policies and gender-neutral housing floors.

Indeed, today's students are no longer reliant on a handful of brochures and a quick campus tour to decide if a college feels right to them. The Internet provides invaluable opportunities to research a potential school, starting with the official website. It can be almost overwhelming to figure out how to wade through all that information to find the few indicators that will make a transgender student feel safe and welcomed at that institution.

So, first, narrow it down. Start at a school's home page, where you will find navigational buttons for incoming and applying students. You won't see any welcome banners for transgender students wishing to apply. But you should note whether the language here stresses diversity, is gender-neutral, and promotes a welcoming attitude for all students. In fact, the word "diversity" itself is a big marker today in more progressive institutions, and it will likely be emphasized repeatedly on the websites of schools that seek a wide span of racial and economic differences and differences in sexual orientation among their students. Also note whether photos on the website visibly reflect this emphasis.

Second, perform keyword searches to find out whether schools have a policy barring discrimination based on sexual orientation and gender identity and expression. As of this writing, according to the Transgender Law and Policy Institute, all the Ivy League colleges and many state and private schools—91 schools in all—have implemented such policies. In fact, this is one of the most important things to look for when considering schools, according to Brett-Genny Janiczek Beemyn, a board member of the Transgender Law and Policy Institute and the Director of the Stonewall Center at the University of Massachusetts at Amherst.

It is important to note, transgender advocates say, that there is often an inconsistency between stated or published policies and actual practices at individual schools. Enrolled students, especially those active in LGBTQ organizations who have been at the school for at least a year or two, will have an idea of this gap between policy and reality. How does the school handle reports of bias and harassment? What progress is the school making on issues that transgender students and their allies have brought up? While the "gender identity and expression" part of the nondiscrimination policy may not have great strength at all the schools which have adopted it, it's worth noting which colleges have at least taken an initial stand on this issue.

Another thing to note is whether the school has a student center or program for LGBTQ students. You can find most centers listed on the website of the National Consortium of Higher Education LGBTQ Resource Professionals, under the Directory tab, at http://www.lgbt campus.org/. It does not list academic programs, so some transgender-friendly schools don't have a listing if they have an academic program but not a student center. Schools that do have a queer center are listed, with a URL and contact information for the staff who run it. Details on these sites should include transgender issues and events, such as Transgender Awareness Day (in November) or even a full week's worth of Transweek activities. If you live near a college that hosts such programming, try to visit during this time. Often such events are open to the public, and you will get a real sense of what the college offers, and who attends, if you can visit in person.

You might also note whether the archived issues of the student newspapers for each college cover transgender issues on campus, and the tone they use to describe transgender students and their allies. Also research the general diversity level and the prevalent attitude toward transgender and LGB people in each town or city you're considering. You may not want to live in hostile territory, even if the school you're considering is progressive.

Checklist for a Transgender-Friendly Campus

__Does the campus designate some restrooms as gender-neutral or provide single-occupancy washrooms? Is there a public list of these somewhere at the school?

__Is there any gender-neutral housing in residence halls?

__Does the school include "sexual orientation" and "gender identity and expression" in its nondiscrimination policies?

__Has the school demonstrated a commitment to hiring and training health care professionals, including mental health counselors, who are knowledgeable about the health care needs of transgender students?

__Are there out, visible, LGB or trans staff and faculty?

__Have forms been revised to allow students to self-identify as transgender?

__Is there staff training for all faculty and staff in ways to keep transgender students safe?

__Are printed and Web materials inclusive of LGBT students, do they celebrate diversity, and do they use gender-neutral language?

__Does the student health center offer hormone therapy?

__Does the school address issues of gender insensitivity or harassment, and does it seem to do this quickly or drag its feet?

__Is there evidence of transgender activism on campus?

Living Arrangements

When looking for a college, transgender students should look for specific steps the school has taken to ensure their comfort and safety. While many of these issues run parallel to issues faced by openly lesbian and gay students, transgender students have their own set of special needs on campus. The first is housing that is safe and comfortable.

Schools that have not kept up with the changes in housing needs may still insist that transgender students live in rooms assigned by their birth gender. Obviously, this will not make for a comfortable college experience. To rectify this, many schools are providing special gender-neutral floors in residence halls. Gender-neutral housing usually means floors or suites where people of all genders can live. Colleges are finding that while most students are very comfortable in these surroundings, some parents of gender-typical students may balk at the medley of folks. Luckily, schools (led by student demands) are forging a path of tolerance by creating these floors or suites, and they usually find takers. When such housing is not available, schools should be able to provide single rooms for accepted students who identify as transgender and will not or cannot live in the available housing options. If no other solution is found, consider off-campus housing if possible.

Hormones and Health Care

More and more universities are covering hormones under their student health plans. According to the Transgender Law and Policy Institute, the list includes Bridgewater State College, Harvard University, Pennsylvania State University, the University of California–Santa Barbara, the Ohio State University, Emerson College, and Suffolk University. Where hormones are not officially covered, some campus doctors provide transgender students with hormones via a diagnosis of "endocrine deficiency" so that hormone replacement therapy can be covered by insurance. If a particular health center will not do so, students tend to network and inform one another of where else hormones can legally be obtained, or even where other supplies like binding wraps can be ordered.

Transgender students have the right to expect health care providers who have been trained to interact with and treat transgender individuals. This includes calling you by your chosen name and not outing you in the waiting room by using a birth name that is obsolete. This level of sensitivity should also extend to your interactions with nurses, staff, and receptionists. However, this is not usually the case; you may need to request trainings for such staff. You can join together with campus LGBTQ organizations to insist upon such trainings.

Resources

Organizations
Transgender Law Center
www.transgenderlawcenter.org

GLSEN (Gay, Lesbian & Straight Education Network)
www.glsen.org/
Works to improve school climate for LGBTQ students.

Gender Spectrum Education and Training
www.genderspectrum.org
Provides training and education about gender diversity to schools and educators.

Gender Public Advocacy Coalition
www.gpac.org/
Works to make all communities, including school communities, safe for everyone, especially those with gender variance.

National Center for Lesbian Rights
www.nclrights.org/
Handles some cases involving school issues.

National Gay and Lesbian Task Force
www.thetaskforce.org/
National organization that does some work for safer schools.

Safe Schools Coalition
www.safeschoolscoalition.org
Works to create safe schools for all LGBT youth.

American Civil Liberties Union
www.aclu.org/
Search the site for current cases involving LGBT youth and school legislation.

GLBT National Help Line
1-800-246-7743

TransProud
www.transproud.com
Networking site for trans youth.

Human Rights Watch: Hatred in the Hallways
http://www.hrw.org/reports/2001/uslgbt/
Based on in-depth interviews with 140 youth and 130 teachers, administrators, counselors, parents, and youth service providers in seven states, this report offers the first comprehensive look at the human rights abuses suffered by lesbian, gay, bisexual, and transgender students.

Books

The Gay and Lesbian Guide to College Life: A Comprehensive Resource for LGBT Students and Their Allies, by John Baez, Jennifer Howd, and Rachel Pepper (Princeton Review, 2007).

The Advocate College Guide for LGBT Students, by Shane Windmeyer (Alyson Publications, 2006).

Websites / Other Resources

http://www.tself.org/

The Transgender Scholarship and Education Legacy Fund, for transgender-identified students in the helping and caring professions.

http://www.campusclimateindex.org

This index enables students and their parents to find detailed information about the policies and practices of schools.

http://www.lgbtcampus.org/

Consortium of higher education LGBT resource professionals, with detailed information on LGBT student programs.

http://www.transgendergenderlaw.org/

The site of the Transgender Law and Policy Institute has a wealth of specific information.

http://www.thepointfoundation.org/

The Point Foundation provides scholarships to college-bound LGBTQ kids and some graduate students.

http://nctequality.org/Resources/Coming_Out_as_Transgender
gender.pdf
 Guidebook written and distributed by the Coming Out Project of the
 Human Rights Campaign and the National Center for Transgender
 Equality: http://nctequality.org/

http://www.glma.org/index.cfm?fuseaction=Page.viewPage&pageID
=692
 Ten things transgender persons should discuss with their health care
 providers.

http://www.nyu.edu/lgbt/transbrochure.pdf
 NYU's health brochure for transgender kids.

Transgeneration, directed by Jeremy Simmons (New Video Group, 2005).
 Two-disc series about four transgender college students.

Chapter 8

Medical Issues for Transgender Children

MOST FAMILIES PLACE A tremendous amount of faith in the opinions and perspectives of their pediatrician or family practice doctor. It is incredibly important to understand that pediatric medical doctors receive little formal training on the subject of gender variance and transgender issues. Times are beginning to change, but widespread systemic change is slow.

Stephanie speaks to pediatricians and pediatric residents on a regular basis, but these are usually elective lectures. And at this point transgender issues are not included in the mandatory curriculum of any medical school in the country. At best, she may be able to provide two hours of training time per school or hospital, during which she has to cover a lot of ground.

In practical terms, this means there is an excellent chance that your child's doctor has never had any training or read anything at all on the subject of transgender children. Your pediatrician may thus bring only their personal opinions and biases, rather than solid, clinical, evidence-based information.

It is important to note that the same is true for child psychiatrists, psychoanalysts, and therapists. Although these professionals have had some training in the unfolding of gender in the young child, the information is limited strictly to norms of expectation, with little to no discussion of natural variation from those norms. Do not assume that the more training or degrees a child psychologist or psychiatrist has, the better they will understand gender variance, or the more likely it is they will treat your child appropriately. Although some progressive schools for therapists are including guest lecturers to cover these issues, they are few and far between. Experts in this field stress that expertise about transgender children is not based on academic degrees, but on the experiences and understanding of individual clinicians.

Additionally, a number of progressive therapists still do not understand that sexual orientation and gender identity are separate parts of core identity. These well-meaning, but misguided, providers try to convince patients (and their parents) that they are actually gay, not transgender or gender-variant. Of course, some of these children are or will be gay. However, gender variance is by no means a definitive marker of sexual orientation. To try to predict a person's sexual orientation in early childhood does little to address the presenting issue of gender variance.

In other words, at this juncture in history it is not an easy task to find a doctor or therapist educated in the issues of gender variance and transgender identity in children and teens. As Dr. Irene Sills, a pediatric endocrinologist, says, the "lack of understanding is enormous" among most pediatricians. Indeed, Jana L. Ekdahl, a therapist who works with transgender children, says that doctors unfamiliar with transgender kids and their care need to treat this as they would any area where they lack experience: "I would recommend that these doctors consult with a gender specialist and/or refer this child to someone who has experience working with gender-variant children." However, many providers erroneously assume that no other provider has this experience either. Thus, a family raising a gender-variant or transgender child must proceed with extreme caution in selecting appropriate care providers.

Despite the lack of knowledge among health care professionals, gender variance in children and teens is a field that is rapidly gaining attention in the media. A tremendous social change is underfoot in regard to understanding biological sex, sexual orientation, gender expression, and gender identity. The national professional conferences for therapists and pediatricians present workshops on these issues, and increasingly positive professional articles are being written on the subject. So don't lose hope. This is a very exciting time of systemic and cultural change. Even though your children and their care providers are trailblazers, know that others will soon follow. For the present, many families find that they are the ones informing their doctors of the latest research and information. Together they are able to bring their care provider up to speed.

Many well-meaning pediatricians and therapists do not realize that their ill-informed recommendations actually increase the stress and potentially increase the short-term and long-term risks for these children. If it has been suggested that you try to discipline the gender variance out of your child, or that you not permit or support their variance, or that your child is too young to know their gender identity, or that you are wrong in supporting their natural gender expression—*these are red flags*. If you have received such messages, it is time to start interviewing other practitioners. The importance of finding an open-minded health care professional cannot be underestimated. Remember, there is an extraordinarily high rate of suicide in transgender and gender-variant teens, and younger children may feel suicidal as well. Seek out a care provider who is aware of this increased risk and is staying updated on the evidence-based research to best help guide you in your parenting and in the medical care of your child.

Although there may not be informed providers in your hometown, it is essential that you find care providers who are at least nonjudgmental and willing to take the time to research the latest information on this subject. By all means, take this book with you to your care providers and prospective care providers. Ask them to read it and investigate the resources provided throughout. Although family doctors do not yet have much experience or training in this field, it is perfectly reasonable to expect your care providers to learn as much as they can when necessary. In fact, many pediatricians are open-minded and astute. If your pediatrician has seen your child for many years, he or she already may have noted in the chart that your child is going by a different name than their birth name, that your child is exhibiting cross-gender behaviors, or even that they have expressed cross-gender feelings. The danger to your family may occur when your primary doctor refers you to a specialist such as a pediatric endocrinologist. If the specialist does not understand or choose to treat transgender children, you may now feel there is nowhere left to go.

Some families are so worried about how their care provider will respond to the child's gender variance that they do not share this information with their doctor. Or they may feel that for routine care such as ear infections or vaccinations, it may not be necessary to divulge. These parents may be a bit ashamed already. Parents usually want to determine for themselves if it is just a phase before talking about it with the doctor. This is not what we recommend. As you are well aware, there is a steep learning curve for understanding and acceptance when it comes to gender variance. Because you have reached the stage where you are reading this book, it is no longer a phase, or it is an extended phase that is having an impact on your lives. Please share this information with your doctor. This will allow your doctor time to become current on the research and medical issues surrounding gender-variant and transgender children. It will also allow you to recognize whether it will be necessary to find another care provider.

> I just realized our pediatrician has not seen my kid in two years, and she is not aware of his transition [from female to male]. I guess

I better make a phone call to assure that she is on board with the gender thing! —Parent of a 7-year-old transboy

As far as what I would have done differently, I would have investigated the doctors I encountered before taking their lame advice. Did they do research? Do they know anything at all about transgender kids? —Parent of an 8-year-old transboy

You may consider scheduling a special parent consultation—without your child—to discuss the issues your family is facing. Come with resources and a positive demeanor. Take careful note of your doctor's responses, including his or her body language. Here is some language that has worked for other families to begin the conversation:

"We know that this issue is a difficult one for many people. But we realize that we need to see a doctor who can help us through this journey without their personal biases influencing the care we receive. It is completely fine with us if, for whatever reason, you do not feel that you would be the best doctor for us. We would really appreciate a recommendation for a different doctor if you have one."

By being direct, you will get a better idea of whether this provider will be able to serve your family's best interests over the long run.

Screening Doctors over the Telephone

You would think that the staff who answer the telephone in a medical office would be aware of their doctors' areas of expertise. This is often not the case. To research this point, Stephanie called three pediatric offices that currently work in a supportive way with young transgender children. She asked if she could consult with the doctor in their practice most familiar with gender issues in children. The receptionists had to ask three or four times what that meant; each time, it was explained to them. Though Stephanie already knew the doctors worked with transgender kids, not one of the offices had staff who knew anything about transgender children. When Stephanie called back with the name of the doctor she knew about, the staff in one office vehemently denied that the doctor would know about such a thing— despite the fact that this doctor and Stephanie had actually met at a workshop two weeks previously and engaged in an informative conversation about this subject.

All this is to say, unfortunately, that you cannot rely on the demeanor, opinions, or perspectives of the office staff as a measure of the knowledge and sensitivity of the practice's providers. Although it creates extra work for you, you will have to schedule in-person or phone appointments with the doctors themselves. This is why networking among families is valuable, and why groups such as Gender Spectrum are in the process of gathering the names of care providers in as many areas as possible who are sensitive to transgender and gender-variant children. If you have found a responsive and caring therapist or medical doctor, please e-mail us at info@genderspectrum.org to add their contact information to the resources available for other families.

Emergency Medicine

Everyone faces the possibility of needing emergency medical services. Unexpected things happen. Here are some things to think about and prepare for in those instances.

At the emergency room, for your child's health insurance to pick up the bill, the child's legal name must appear on their chart. If you have a transgender child who has not had a legal name change, inform the staff in this way: "This is my child, David Nancy Carson." If you have been seen there before, you may have to add, "You probably have her in the system as Nancy Carson, but she goes by David—please add that to your system." When it is time for him to be seen, they will call "David," and your child won't be outed in the waiting room.

If it is an urgent medical situation that does not involve your child's genitals—such as a broken arm—and your child has not yet gone through puberty, you may not need to tell the medical providers anything. They will call your child "David" as they put the cast on his arm. If they do look more closely at the chart (unlikely for a broken arm), you can sometimes pass off a question such as "Why did you name him Nancy?" by saying, "It's a long story." You do not have a responsibility to reveal this information. There is no falsification in using your child's preferred name or pronoun, or in not bringing up their gender status to a medical provider when obtaining emergency medical services. You can play it by ear, deciding in the moment if it is relevant to disclose your child's transgender status.

If you do determine there is a need to disclose it, and there is time and space to do so, ask the medical staff to step outside with you while you explain the situation to them. This saves your child the embarrassment of this disclosure and the possible confused reaction of the doctor. Now may be an appropriate time to tell the doctor that, since it is not relevant to the current injury, you would appreciate the gender issue not being discussed, as it is private and personal.

At any point, it is your right to ask any of the staff to refrain from questioning your child about their gender or making negative remarks or comments. If needed, be clear and direct about the respect you expect. If they continue, you can always request a new nurse or doctor to care for your child. You must be your child's advocate.

On the other hand, it is not always so easy. If you live in or are traveling in an area where you think you may face serious discrimination because your child's gender is not what it seems, it is best to be prepared. If possible, obtain a notarized letter from your doctor stating that your child is transgender, and keep a copy in your car and in your wallet (and in your child's wallet, if they are old enough). This will curtail problems such as calls made to Child Protective Services in confusion. We include an example of such a letter in Appendix 2.

If your child is under the care of an endocrinologist or other doctor for the administration of cross-hormones, consider having your child wear a medical ID bracelet as a way of validating this medical "condition" that may come up in an unrelated medical situation. The bracelet can give generic information only—staff must call the phone number to access the child's medical information, and an operator provides the information from the child's prescribing doctor, including the confidential nature of the information.

What Is GID?

If you have a child who is gender-variant or transgender, you will hear the term *gender identity disorder,* or GID, quite frequently. The term is used by the medical profession and appears in the Diagnostic and Statistical Manual of Mental Disorders, or DSM-IV. For doctors or mental health professionals to make an official diagnosis of gender identity disorder, five criteria must be met, including evidence of a strong, often overwhelming, cross-gender identification—also called *gender dysphoria.* Gender dysphoria is usually experienced from childhood on, and it is not based on any cultural preference but on a person's innate sense of self: it is characterized by persistent discomfort and distress about one's assigned sex or gender, including socially and occupationally. There can be no evidence of any intersex condition in relation to the diagnosis of GID. (See the sidebar titled What about Intersex People? in Chapter 1.)

It is important to note that not all transgender people feel that the definition of GID reflects how they feel about their identity. Likewise, many people do not believe that being transgender is a "mental disorder," and they want GID to be reconsidered, and possibly removed from classification in the DSM, as homosexuality was in 1973. Until GID is removed from the DSM, being transgender will be seen as a psychiatric condition and not a medical condition. A GID diagnosis allows for insurance coverage for psychotherapy, but it effectively prevents insurance coverage for gender-related medical care.

Do Transgender and Gender-variant Children Need Therapy?

This question needs to be answered from several different but equally important perspectives. First, what are the needs of your child. Second, how can parents in conflict over the appropriate way to raise their child make supportive decisions for their child. Third, how can parents protect themselves from outsiders who determine that their choices are morally wrong and call Child Protective Services. Finally, how can families prepare for the possibility that their child will use medications to delay puberty or to develop secondary sex characteristics of their chosen gender, rather than their natal, or birth, sex. We will cover these considerations in this section.

Children and teens who are gender-variant experience differing degrees of stress around their nonconformity. Much of this stress is caused by society's lack of acceptance and understanding about gender variance and transgender identity and expression. Thus, gender-variant people experience negative self-reflection from those around them on a daily basis.

> *The onset of puberty was when my kid's sullen behavior started. This was our kid who from age 12, when the testosterone started flowing, knew a big error had been made. The preoccupation, the distractibility, the retreat into his own world of trying to figure out what made him feel so different from everyone else.* —Parent of a 20-year-old transwoman

> *My family and I have been in therapy to get more information about being trans. I still go, but my mom, who is pretty supportive, stopped going. I find it very helpful. I have been going for more than three years now, since I started transitioning at 14.* —17-year-old transboy

Society is not at ease with gender variance. This lack of acceptance from others causes a cascade of internal reactions and responses for the child. It can be difficult to differentiate between preexisting or coexisting conditions and stress reactions caused by the gender issues. For example, a number of children and teens present in therapy with problems such as posttraumatic stress disorder, obsessive-compulsive disorder, anxiety disorders, bullying behaviors, and withdrawal or suicidal tendencies. Some therapists want to treat these conditions to see if the gender issues disappear. However, it is much more common for these issues to disappear once the gender dysphoria is addressed. In numerous cases, most or all of the coexisting diagnoses are removed after children are allowed to live in accordance with their gender identity or to express their gender in the ways that feel most natural to them.

Likewise, if your child is treated by a misinformed therapist, they may be wrongly diagnosed as having bipolar disorder or another psychiatric condition, or they may be subjected to harmful reparative therapy to try to reorient them to their birth gender.

On the other hand, good therapy can be a huge blessing for your child and your family. An experienced therapist can help your child unwind their internal shame and increase their self-esteem and resiliency, especially in the face of ridicule from others. A good therapist can also help your child with the self-blame they may feel for the increased stress in your family's life due to their gender expression or identity. Furthermore, a therapist who explores a child's feelings of body dysphoria may be able to reduce the likelihood of self-mutilation.

Protecting Your Family

Another very important reason to consider a therapist for your child is to protect your family. Transgender and gender-variant expression is still not widely understood in our society. As a result, some people are likely to think that you are causing your child great harm by supporting them. Finding a reputable therapist to work with your family will validate your choices in the face of adversity.

Even though it may make the most sense for your child to see a transgender therapist, many families initially choose a typically gendered therapist who has a strong grasp of gender issues. By doing so they avoid the possibility of having an "agenda" for their child.

If you are separated from your child's other legal parent, or if there is tension between you on the subject of your child's gender expression and identity, it is especially important for your child to see a therapist. In addition to providing guidance for your family, the therapist can also validate that neither the supportive parent nor the rejecting parent is driving the child to express themselves in this way. Neither of you has caused your child to be gender-variant, nor is anyone to blame for your child's innate gender identity.

If you are having a hard time with your child's other parent around the way you are handling your child's gender variance, you run a significant risk that they will make a move for legal custody. To protect yourself in this eventuality, it is best that the child's pediatrician refer your

The AMA and Gender Identity

In 2007, the Board of Trustees of the American Medical Association (AMA) amended its policies to include language that would prohibit discrimination against and ensure "protection and equality relating to gender identity issues." The AMA's policy now states: "Physicians cannot refuse to care for patients based on gender identity." The AMA also opposes the denial of health insurance on the basis of sexual orientation or gender identity. Doctors who do not comply can be admonished, censured, or even lose their licenses. This very strong message from the AMA will reverberate greatly throughout the medical community and eventually have a positive effect on care for transgender people of all ages.

child to a therapist with a gender specialty. That way, the neutral parties in your life are guiding the course of care, and it cannot appear as if you are diagnosing your child yourself.

Preparing for Future Medical Care

Although there are currently no standards regulating children's mental health care and access to transgender medicines, that could change at any time. It would be a shame if you and your child got to the point of feeling ready to proceed with hormones only to find out there was now a rule requiring two years of therapy prior to receiving cross-hormones. If your child is under the care of a mental health professional, you and your provider can decide jointly how frequently your child should be seen—weekly, monthly, or even less frequently. But it is advisable to have a therapist on board prior to the teenage years, with an eye to the potential future care of your child.

Medical Options

In the following sections we discuss the medical options for transgender children, including puberty-delaying medications and delaying puberty with cross-hormones—the sex hormones (testosterone or estrogen) of the child's affirmed, not biological, sex.

Delaying Puberty

Parents of transgender children may want to delay the onset of their child's puberty to prevent any unwanted results of birth-sex puberty from permanently altering their child's body. Delaying puberty is also a means of putting body development on hold in children who have recently expressed a transgender identity, so the family can buy time to figure out what is truly going on with the child.

The medical term for drugs that delay puberty is *GnRH inhibitors,* or *GnRH analogues.* Many families call these medicines "blockers." GnRH inhibitors can be administered to a child of either sex. They shut down the newly awakened adolescent hormonal surges and effectively stop a child's pubertal development. This delay is fully reversible—if a child discontinues the use of GnRH inhibitors, even if they have been on the medicines for several years, the body resumes its natural course in about six months, picking up developmentally where it left off. After the medicines are discontinued, the child's development lags initially but eventually catches up. The bodily changes resume their normal and natural progression, as if they had not been put on hold.

Although in the US GnRH inhibitors have not been used for very long with transgender children, the Dutch have had much success using them in this fashion. In the Netherlands, where socialized medicine entitles everyone to health care, there is an established protocol for working with persistently cross-gender children. These medicines have been used in the US during the past 30 years for children experiencing "precocious puberty"—children whose development starts inappropriately early—to delay their puberty until a more appropriate age. In all cases where this medicine has been used with children in the Netherlands and the US, there has been no indication that it is unsafe for puberty to be delayed in the human body. Likewise, the delay of puberty has no obvious impact on future fertility, nor has it led to an increase in birth defects in the offspring of people who were administered these medicines as children.

According to Dr. Norman Spack of the Gender Management Service (GeMS) Clinic at Children's Hospital Boston, a growing number of doctors working internationally with transgender children—in the US, the Netherlands, Britain, Belgium, and Norway—have now agreed to standardize their intake screenings using psychological testing for gender identity with gender-variant and affirmed transgender children. This will better ensure that all medical facilities undertake the same screening of their clients, allow better statistic gathering, and potentially implement an agreed-upon set of protocols. As intake screenings become more standardized, the participating doctors believe, statistics will show that few affirmed transgender children change their minds about their affirmed gender identity as they grow up, or regret having sought early treatment.

Much anguish can be prevented if younger transgender teenagers 12 or 13 years old are allowed to begin hormonal therapy at Tanner stage 2 (see sidebar titled The Tanner Stages), instead of making them wait until they are 16 or 17, when they have progressed further and more permanently through the puberty of their birth sex. Moreover, such guidelines for early treatment could be used to convince insurance companies to cover the cost of the most effective medication, even if it

The Tanner Stages

Puberty for both males and females is divided into five broad stages known as the Tanner stages. Stage 1 is prepuberty. Stage 2 is the early signs of puberty, such as the first appearance of breast buds in girls at around age 11–12, and testicular growth in boys at around age 12–14. Stages 3–4 are marked by continuing development, and stage 5 is full adult development. Dr. Norman Spack of the GeMS Clinic suggests that the only way to accurately assess a child's development is to have the child examined by a physician trained in the subtleties of the Tanner stages. This is especially critical if there is any discussion about a child beginning hormonal blocker treatment. Few people outside the medical profession have heard of the Tanner stages, but the stages become relevant when puberty-delaying medications are prescribed. In the Netherlands, puberty-delaying medications are often started at Tanner stage 2. This is part of what is known as the "Dutch protocol." More information on the Tanner stages can be found in medical textbooks or online.

is expensive, and may influence such guidelines set forth by organizations such as WPATH. (See sidebar titled What Is WPATH?) For more on this research, including the differences between the Dutch protocol and that of other countries, go to: www.gires.org.uk/Web_Page_ Assets/Hormonal_Medication.htm#Developing.

Considerations Regarding Delaying Puberty

GnRH inhibitors put the body's development on hold, preventing the experience of the growth spurts of puberty and keeping the child's body prepubertal. As a result, for the duration of treatment, your child may be significantly shorter than their peers and appear younger. Keep in mind, however, that many children are late bloomers—if you walk through the halls of any middle school or high school you will see a wide range of physical development in the kids.

Another consideration in delaying puberty is cognitive development. While your child is being treated with GnRH inhibitors, your child will not experience the cognitive development that comes naturally with the increase of hormonal activity in the body. Once again, this is simply a delay and not a permanent condition. As far as is known, choosing to administer these medicines has no permanent impact on development.

On the flip side, it is also important to consider that estrogen and testosterone create permanent and semipermanent changes in a developing body. If you choose not to administer these medicines to delay puberty in your transgender child, you are dramatically increasing the likelihood of future surgeries for your child. This may be especially true for biological males, since the effects of testosterone on structural development are more permanent than those of estrogen.

Let's explain this. When a body undergoes the changes brought on by estrogen, the hips widen, the breasts grow, the menstrual cycle starts, the skin softens, and fat is distributed to places like the hips. These changes "feminize" a person—allowing us to recognize them as female. When a body undergoes the changes brought on by testosterone, the voice deepens, the hair growth patterns permanently alter to include growth on the face, chest, arms, and back, the shoulders widen, the Adam's apple develops, and the bone structure of the face changes. These changes "virilize" a person—allowing us to recognize them as male. Much of the impact of testosterone is irreversible. This makes it difficult for a body that has been virilized ever to be seen as fully female—even after administering estrogen—without multiple surgical alterations.

Because testosterone is such a dominant hormone, a body that has naturally gone through female puberty can be given testosterone and easily transform into a body that is seen as male. The resulting person may be a short male with breasts, but the testosterone brings with it the needed changes for that person to be widely perceived as male. Breasts can be easily hidden, or they can be surgically removed at a later date in a single operation. A body that has undergone male puberty can be given estrogen to effect some changes, but expensive surgeries will be needed for facial reconstruction and the lessening of the Adam's apple, often called a tracheal shave. Extensive electrolysis and voice retraining will also likely be necessary. And nothing can be done about a person's height or bone size, post-adolescence. As a result, many transgender women (anatomical males who identify as female) who were not given puberty-delaying medicines are forever recognized as being transgender and are not perceived as female.

> My child has been on hormones for over three years. She intends to have more facial therapy within the next year and SRS thereafter, but money is a huge issue. I wish blockers had been available when she was young. —Parent of a 22-year-old transwoman

Now, the goal is not always necessarily to "pass" as the other sex. But as parents of transgender children and teens, the choices you make about their medical options at this point will have a great impact on their future. By allowing your child or teen to delay puberty, or to use cross-hormones (discussed below), you are ensuring a greater likelihood that your child will not be discriminated against based purely on appearance. This improves their job opportunities as well as their personal safety in the world, not to mention their self-esteem and body image.

Cost Considerations and Insurance Coverage

Whether or not your child will be covered for some or all of the medicines pertaining to their transgender health care depends on your insurance plan. Each insurance company has different plans and policies. It is important to check to see what your policy covers. Look through the exclusions. Some insurance plans actually cover transgender health care needs; others do not. If you have the option to change insurance plans, make sure to do this research, and then you can advocate for expanding their coverage. While many insurance companies do not cover hormonal therapy for children or adults, some do. When billing insurance companies, many doctors use a variety of different diagnoses related to hormonal imbalances or unwanted pubertal changes. Currently, the city of San Francisco and a growing handful of companies in California require their health insurance carriers to cover transgender health care, including surgeries.

If your insurance company does not cover the cost of puberty-delaying medications for transgender children and teens, they will be expensive—very expensive. Dr. Norman Spack currently estimates the cost at around $500–$600 a month, and these costs will likely be incurred for at least several years. Hormones and some implants and injections, Spack suggests, can run up to $15,000 a year. We have heard from Canadian therapists that the cost of these medications is dramatically cheaper in Canada. We hope the high out-of-pocket costs for these meds will decline soon.

We knew we had to do something. Our child needed these medicines. It was not a hard decision to make for each of us to get second jobs.

Our child feels very bad about us working so much for him. We just look at him and tell him he is beautiful, he is our son. We will do anything for him. It is not him that is the problem, it is the insurance company and the culture that just don't understand that there is nothing wrong with him. We love him just the way God made him. If he says he's a boy living in this body, that's the truth. —Parent of a 10-year-old transboy

GnRH Inhibitors in Greater Detail

GnRH inhibitors, or "blockers," such as the brand Lupron, prevent the pituitary gland at the base of the brain from signaling to the ovaries and testes to produce the sex hormones estrogen and testosterone, thereby allowing a pre-pubescent child to hold off puberty. Blockers, according to pediatric endocrinologist Dr. Irene Sills, can be "a way of sticking a toe into the water, without going for a swim" in the sea of hormones. Originally prescribed to children with early or "precocious" puberty, blockers act on a naturally occurring hormone called gonadotropin-releasing hormone, or GnRH.

These drugs keep the child in a physical holding pattern until the child, the parents, and doctors can agree on a future course of treatment. GnRH inhibitors can be administered by intramuscular injection every one to three months, by nasal spray, or as an annual implant. There are no conclusive studies on their long-term use, but to date no studies show adverse effects after a few years of use. Talk to a well-informed doctor about what medications, if any, are best for your child.

It was such a relief. I wish I could have started testosterone right away. But my parents told me that they really needed me to be sure of the choices I was making. I was sure. I have always been sure. But they needed some time. I can understand that. —11-year-old transboy

Pediatric Endocrinologists

Why do pediatric endocrinologists end up treating transgender children? Because these specialists, in the words of Dr. Irene Sills, "know how to put kids through puberty." The flip side of this, Dr. Norman Spack adds, is that endocrinologists "also know how to block puberty." Whether by prescribing and administering hormones or otherwise advising on the medical treatment for kids who wish to delay puberty, receive hormones, or change their gender, endocrinologists are the experts. But, Dr. Sills reminds parents, treating transgender children is "not just about hormones."

I am on testosterone now, and I have thought about surgery. I plan on getting that all done when I get the money for it. —17-year-old transboy

Finding a Doctor to Administer Puberty-Delaying Medicines

There are doctors who are working with families to delay puberty in transgender children. The number is small, but growing. Many families travel long distances to get the health care they need for their child—in some instances to another state, or even to other countries. Pediatric endocrinologists who are supportive of treatment for transgender youth are trying to change this. They're presenting at national conferences and encouraging their peers to consider providing such services in their practices. As more and more practitioners educate themselves about how to administer the medications and how to care for children who are transgender, there will be a significant increase in the number of doctors administering such medicines.

Dr. Irene Sills, pediatric endocrinologist, believes that all pediatricians could be easily trained to safely administer both GnRH inhibitors and cross-hormones to their child and teen patients. "It's time for other doctors to step up to the plate," she says.

Most doctors administering medical treatments to transgender children impose certain requirements before starting any treatment. Currently, most doctors require parental consent and a mental health evaluation. In some practices, only one parent's consent is required; in others, all legal parents must consent. Requirements relating to mental health vary widely. Some doctors require that a therapist affiliated with their practice conduct a mental health screening of all family members to verify that the child is clear and unwavering about their transgender status, that there are no prohibiting mental health diagnoses, and that the child is not being pressured to make unwanted changes to their body. In other practices, the family need only bring a letter from the child's therapist documenting that the child is clearly transgender. Some doctors require that a child have lived in the world in accordance with their gender identity prior to administering GnRH inhibitors. Most do not.

Medical doctors do not want to be responsible for assessing the mental health of their patients. But they usually want to know if an assessment has already been made by another professional. According to Dr. Irene Sills, a pediatric endocrinologist will probably want to see a record of at least a year of therapy to feel secure that hormone therapy is the correct next step in a transgender teen's care, but this extended course of therapy is not required in order to administer puberty-delaying medications. Thus the family can put their child's body on hold for pubertal changes while exploring more deeply, in therapy, the implications of administering cross-hormones.

Many parents feel frustrated by the mental health components of their child's care. But do not let these considerations delay your child's access to care. It is certainly reasonable to ask for a deeper assessment before making permanent changes to your child's body by administering cross-hormones. But if you wish simply to delay puberty, you should be able

What Is WPATH?

The World Professional Association for Transgender Health, referred to as WPATH, was formerly known as the Harry Benjamin International Gender Dysphoria Association, Inc. WPATH is a professional organization devoted to the understanding and treatment of gender identity disorders. It is an international, interdisciplinary professional organization comprising pediatricians, therapists, surgeons, and others who work with transgender people of all ages. The mission of WPATH is to "further the understanding and treatment of gender identity disorders by professionals in medicine, psychology, law, social work, counseling, psychotherapy, family studies, sociology, anthropology, sexology, speech and voice therapy, and other related fields." The organization's website, www.wpath.org, is largely accessible to members only.

What Are the Standards of Care?

WPATH publishes a volume titled *Standards of Care for Gender Identity Disorders,* which is the organization's "professional consensus about the psychiatric, psychological, medical, and surgical management of gender identity disorders." Not all professionals working with transgender people agree completely with the provisions of the Standards, and revisions are commonplace in individual practices. However, the Standards remain the most official doctrine for professionals and researchers in transgender care. The first edition was published in 1979; the current edition is the sixth. It is available in English and Spanish versions from this site: http://www.wpath.org/publicationsstandards.cfm.

to find a provider who will prescribe the medicines in a timely manner with only a brief assessment.

Cross-hormones

Because transgender people often want to be perceived by others as they perceive themselves, many choose the option of taking cross-hormones to visibly change their bodies. Plenty of transgender individuals do not choose to alter their bodies with medicines or surgeries. Some transgender individuals would like to use cross-hormones but are not able to due to preexisting medical or mental health considerations. There is no "right way" to be transgender. This is really important for parents to understand. The goal is not for your child to appear in a way that makes you feel comfortable; the goal is for your child to feel as comfortable as they can in their body. The choice to make any physical alterations to their body should be up to them and not spurred on by their parents, doctor, therapist, or other family members.

Some of the changes that happen to the body from the administration of cross-hormones are permanent, and some are not. This is a fairly complex issue that warrants further research on your part.

Cross-hormones can be given to stop, and in some cases reverse, the characteristics of one's birth sex. According to Dr. Irene Sills, hormones are needed to "stop the child's puberty in the wrong gender and allow them to go forward in puberty with the right gender." Estrogen is given to female-identified children to feminize their bodies. Testosterone is given to male-identified children to virilize their bodies. These hormones stimulate the development of the physical and emotional characteristics of one's affirmed gender. As Jana Ekdahl, a gender specialist, writes, "This option offers the adolescent an opportunity to feel happier and more congruent, which in turn helps create a positive high school experience for them, especially in the social arena." If teens are allowed to take cross-hormones (particularly after taking hormone blockers first), they develop many characteristics of the other sex, including facial and body bone structure, voice pitch, growing of breasts (in male-to-female transition), possibly increased height, and the growth of facial and body hair (in female-to-male transition). Hormone shots are given by injection and can be administered by a doctor or the patient. Other ways of administering hormone therapy include gels, patches, nasal sprays, testosterone pellets inserted under the skin, and weekly subcutaneous injections. Injections, Dr. Norman Spack says, are "the most effective way of suppressing menstrual flow."

Anatomical Males

If your biological boy child never developed past early Tanner stage 2 before taking GnRH inhibitors, and starts using estrogen while on GnRH inhibitors, your child will experience only female puberty. In other words, male puberty is stopped, and as estrogen is introduced, female puberty begins. As long as the estrogen is continued, your child will experience only female puberty, with the resulting feminization. Indeed, your child's previously male body will soften and develop breasts, the voice will not deepen, and the hair growth will not masculinize. The muscles and fat will have a female appearance. Of course, your child will never menstruate, having a male reproductive anatomy. The only thing "male" about your child's body will be the genitalia. It is advisable that the estrogen and GnRH inhibitors be continued together until the testes are removed. We discuss surgeries later in the chapter.

Fertility Considerations

If your child's previously male body, as described above, continues on cross-hormones and estrogen together, never going through male puberty, it will never produce sperm.

Sperm are only produced after the body has undergone male pubertal changes. Technically, while a body still has testes it is capable of producing sperm. Certainly, transgender women (biological males who identify as female) who undergo male puberty before taking estrogen may be able to produce sperm in the future. In Stephanie's other life as a midwife, she has worked with a number of transwomen in this circumstance who want to procreate. To do so, they must discontinue estrogen altogether. Over time, and with guidance, they can restore their sperm count to a level that may permit them to impregnate a female-bodied partner via intrauterine insemination or in vitro fertilization—even though their sperm count may still be in the technically sterile range. When the estrogen is discontinued, their bodies naturally virilize. As one might imagine, these transwomen do not enjoy the process of their body virilizing after having taken such care to feminize their bodies.

Taking this a step farther into uncharted territory, a biologically male child who has not gone through puberty could take GnRH inhibitors, then estrogen, and then decide as an adult that she wants to produce sperm. In theory, after being off of all medicines for six months, the body would start to undergo male puberty. In theory, there is a possibility that the body would then, over time, produce sperm, though there is no guarantee these sperm would be fertile. Therefore, according to current thinking, the choice to progress from GnRH inhibitors to estrogen without fully experiencing male puberty should be viewed as giving up one's fertility, and the family and child should be counseled accordingly.

Some parents consider delaying the use of puberty blockers until the child is old enough to produce sperm, so their child will be able to bank sperm before beginning this medical regime. But here are some other things to consider: Most young, anatomically male teenagers who feel they are girls would not, in their worst nightmare, go to a sperm bank to donate sperm, let alone do so on the numerous occasions required to bank sufficient sperm. And most important, remember that there are many, many ways to create family—allowing your child to forgo their fertility does not mean forgoing becoming a parent, should they later wish to become one. If your transgender daughter fantasizes about becoming a parent, it is about becoming a mother—not a biological father. Forcing their body to virilize in order to preserve the theoretical possibility of a biological child will create permanent, unwanted changes in their body and will likely have a serious impact on their relationship with you.

For anatomical males who take estrogen, the results are largely reversible. If they discontinue taking estrogen at some point in the future, their body's natural testosterone will take over again. The breasts will recede, and the feminine fat and muscle will redistribute to male patterns. However, if the testes have been removed, the body will not produce enough testosterone on its own to reverse the feminization. Likewise, if other surgeries have been performed, the body will still reflect the effects of those surgeries.

Anatomical Females
A biological girl child who uses GnRH inhibitors prior to breast development and prior to menstruation, and then begins cross-hormone testosterone, will go through male puberty only. This is very important to understand. Your child will actually develop a male body. Granted, the genitals will still be female, but your child will not develop breasts; he will grow hair on the face and chest, his voice will deepen, he will develop male muscle mass, and he will have a male sex drive. He may experience bouts of intense feelings of anger or euphoria related to the testosterone. His genitals will change as well; the clitoris will lengthen to the size of a very small penis. These changes are much more substantial and dramatic if the body did not become feminized first.

Fertility Considerations
A female body is born with all the eggs it will ever have. However, those eggs do not mature until the body goes through female puberty. It is only after the body starts to ovulate that its eggs are ready for fertilization. This means that if your anatomical female child uses GnRH inhibitors prior to menstruation and regular ovulation, the female reproductive

organs are still undeveloped. Currently there is not a way to surgically remove the eggs at this stage for use in the future. That is possible only after the body is allowed to go through puberty: about a year after the first period, the child can be administered medications to mature her eggs and have them removed and stored. This procedure is extremely expensive, and finding a fertility clinic willing to perform this on a child under 18 is probably impossible.

To preserve your anatomical female child's fertility, it is necessary for your child to go through female puberty. To ensure the safety of the fetus, it would be best for your child not to take testosterone at all until after a pregnancy. After fertility, your transmale child could stay off hormones until legal adulthood (age 18) and then choose to harvest and freeze the eggs for use in the future. If the eggs are harvested in this way, your son could then use these eggs, with sperm from a sperm donor, to impregnate his female partner or a surrogate mother via in vitro fertilization. Just as with anatomical males, if your child took GnRH inhibitors and testosterone before going through puberty and later discontinued both medications, it is possible their body would resume where it left off in female puberty development. In this case, the body would maintain its male appearance but would begin to grow breasts, redistribute fat, and menstruate. Keep in mind that it would probably require a full 18 months off testosterone before pregnancy was possible, and many individuals are not able to achieve pregnancy at that point, or ever. Therefore, as in biological males, it is perhaps best to think of the choice to use GnRH inhibitors and cross-hormones as a choice to relinquish fertility.

In her capacity as a midwife, Stephanie has worked with a number of transmen (biological females who identify as male) who decide to bear children after having been on testosterone. This can be a long and complicated process. Suffice it to say that it may take quite a while to resume a rhythmic menstrual cycle, and there are resultant fertility issues, including an enormously high rate of polycystic ovarian syndrome. No research has been done on the possible increase in children's birth defects resulting from transmen taking testosterone prior to pregnancy, but based on anecdotal evidence, the incidence is higher.

Although this issue of fertility is often huge for parents, it does not loom so large for teens. Reproductive freedom for transgender teens may mean freedom from ever having to think of these issues. If and when they do decide to parent, they conceptualize it differently from their parents, according to family therapist Reid Vanderburgh, who works with many families of transgender kids. Indeed, he says, "Parents will find that their trans son envisions himself as a father when he considers parenting, not as a mother, and vice versa for trans daughters. The parents I've worked with then have been able to more fully accept that the urge to transition overrides the desire to have a biological child, because the child's need to transition is a driving force long before a child is old enough to feel any desire to reproduce." And yes, it is possible that your child may later regret the choices they made when younger. But you will make these choices together—doing the absolute best that you can.

Double Puberty: Wasn't the First Time Enough?

If your child does not use GnRH inhibitors, and you allow them at some point to administer cross-hormones, you are in a very unique position as a parent: having to live with your child through two puberties—one of each gender! Parents who have had this experience often feel emotionally exhausted after a solid stretch of pubertal changes. Our recommendation to you as a parent is this: take your vitamins and hunker down for the hormonal ride!

"No Ho's"

It may be of interest to parents to know that a growing number of teens who identify as transgender and genderqueer refer to themselves by the term *no ho's,* for "no hormones." They are choosing not to change their bodies—instead, they want to change the world. And they may not be quite ready to define themselves. As Dr. Harvey Makadon of Harvard University says, "There is a trend among some young people not to specifically define their sexuality or gender." Please remember that it is essential that your teen be exposed to many different ways of being trans-gender and genderqueer. Attending the Gender Spectrum Family and Youth conference is a great way to do this: it brings teens from across the country together to talk about what's important to them. A gather-ing such as this allows them to see that everyone makes different choices about what is right for them. Your child may want to live in their body just as it is. It does not make their transgender identity any less valid than another child's choice to take hormones or undergo surgery.

Surgeries

All transgender surgeries—except genital reconstruction—are avoided by using GnRH inhibitors and cross-hormones. This is a compelling argument, in and of itself, for the use of puberty blockers.

Before we explain genital surgery in more detail, we want to point out that genital reconstruction is an extremely personal decision. Some transgender people feel it is critically important to their self-experience, whereas others feel that they are fine with their original set of genitals. There is no "right way" to think about genital surgery.

It is very important to realize that many transgender people who elect to have genital surgery do not retain genital sexual sensation. Youth who have limited sexual experience cannot understand fully what they would be giving up by undergoing surgery. Many transgender adults who do not choose surgery strongly advise parents not to think of genital surgery as the only goal of transition.

Although a child generally cannot consent to any surgeries on their own (see sidebar titled Health Care Consent for Children Under 18), with the permission of their parents teens can have surgeries at any age as long as the surgeon is willing. This means that testes can be removed even if genital reconstruction surgery is delayed. There is great advantage to removing testes: it greatly reduces the amount of cross-hormones a child needs to override the testosterone their body is producing. Teenage transboys can have their breasts removed, a surgery that increasing numbers of surgeons are willing to do on teenagers over 16. These two surgeries, while they require recovery time and may involve some complications, are very desirable in the eyes of most trans teens.

The "lower" surgeries—genital reconstructive surgeries—are much bigger deals. They are extremely expensive, and they create significant changes in the body. Many, many transgender adults do not choose these surgeries. By the time they are adults they are better able to understand the sexual trade-off for changing their bodies in this way. As a result, most parents feel it is best for their child to grow out of the teenage years and into adulthood before permanently altering their bodies.

How Do I Make Medical Decisions about and for My Child?

I'll never forget the first time he asked how old he has to be before he can have his "pee-pee" cut off. —Grandparent of a gender-variant 6-year-old boy

It is very hard for any parent of a transgender child or teen to make medical decisions about and for their child. For some parents the medical choices represent a final frontier of sorts—an obvious marker that the change is permanent and that you are acknowledging it as such. However, if your child has been living in accordance with their gender identity already, and seems comfortable, the decisions become clearer. The longer your child has been cross-gender, and the longer you have had to consider the options, the easier it is to come to peace with them. Medical intervention can be a more difficult decision when your preteen or teen suddenly announces they are transgender. This news is almost always shocking and difficult to integrate.

A teen, in the midst of puberty, can understandably feel a strong sense of urgency as a result of their recent physical changes. There can be intense pressure to make potentially permanent decisions without enough time or adequate understanding. As a parent, your goal is to support your child while taking the time to make thoughtful, informed decisions. Navigating this terrain without alienating your child can be very difficult even in the best of circumstances.

Facilitating physical changes for transgender children—referred to as *transitioning* (see Chapter 5, Transition Decisions)—brings new questions about ethics, religion, fertility, and nature. As a parent learns more, some fears may be allayed while new fears are inspired. Parents may grieve for the dreams they had for their child, and may not yet have discovered new ones to take their place. Yet, for these children, the opportunity for their bodies to develop in the way that feels most natural to them is one of the most affirming times of their lives.

The importance of family support during this transition cannot be underestimated. Take time to let your child know that you support them. Keep the lines of communication open, and explore options together. Discussing what you learn together keeps the whole family better informed and allows for ample adjustment time. However, keep in mind that a parent and a child may have very different ideas of an appropriate timetable. Your child may feel rejected by you if these critical life decisions are delayed indefinitely.

During this time of medical decision making, it is not uncommon for families to experience internal conflict and contention. It is an excellent time for families to get supportive counseling and assistance in making these complicated decisions. And please remember that even though it may feel very drastic, by allowing your child to take GnRH inhibitors you are buying yourself and your child needed time.

Can Teens Make Their Own Decisions?

There are some important things to remember about teens. If you say no too strongly to something that feels like life or death for them, it may well mean the difference between life and death to them. This is so heavy to think about, but with gender-variant and transgender teenagers it's a heartbreaking reality. If you say no to hormones, they can and will find them on the street. These hormones may not be clean, and your child will not be under the care of a doctor, and no one will be monitoring their dosage or side effects.

Legally, children can become emancipated minors. If you give them their freedom, they can legally make these decisions on their own, and doctors can treat them legally. If you are unable to consent to their treatment, and you realize you are running the risk that they will run away or obtain street drugs, consider letting them go, legally. Contact the Sylvia

---

Health Care Consent for Children Under 18

Many doctors are reluctant to give hormones to, or perform surgery on, teenagers under 18. The Sylvia Rivera Law Project, which works on behalf of transgender people, states, "A parent, guardian, or the state can consent to health care for people under 18. Health care providers may treat young people for gender identity issues—including with hormones—if a parent, guardian, or foster care agency agrees." Further, teenagers can consent to all of their own care if they are emancipated, or sometimes if "a parent or guardian has refused to give consent and a doctor finds that treatment is necessary and in your best interest." This includes the administration of hormones to youths over 16; while less likely, it may also include surgery. Visit the website for more complete details: www.srlp.org.

Rivera Law project for more information. (See the sidebar titled Health Care Consent for Children Under 18.)

Ongoing Health Care for Your Transgender Teen

If your teen is transgender or significantly gender-variant (whether or not they are taking hormones), you need to find a doctor who respects them and can talk to them about their general and specific health care needs. If you have not found such a doctor in your area, consider traveling to a major metropolitan area that has a clinic for queer youth. The experience of having a health care provider acknowledge your teen's pronouns and ask relevant questions about their sexuality can provide a boost to their self-esteem that will last a long, long time.

It is essential that your teen get good counseling and current information regarding safe sex practices and sexually transmitted disease screening, Pap smears, and birth control information. Often, parents are uncomfortable just talking to their children about sex and sexuality. Having a transgender child may complicate even the best-intentioned parent's ability to speak knowledgeably and sensitively with their child about sex (including safe sex), intimacy, and relationships. The Internet is an excellent source of information and support for gender-variant teens, and some trans or queer youth organizations are able to provide adult mentors who can speak with your child about issues they may have. But it is also important for your teen to know that they have an actual medical provider they can turn to who can give them the care and information they deserve. This is a concrete way you can help your child. You can prescreen doctors to assess their comfort and familiarity with the subjects of gender and sex. You can arrange for the doctors or health clinics in your area to get appropriate training so that they can serve the needs of your child. One source of information is a college or university, if there is one in your area. College campuses often have a general or LGBT-specific health center that could see your child as an outpatient or help you determine where to take them.

A Visit to a Gender Clinic

In February 2007, Dr. Norman Spack, an endocrinologist, and Dr. David Diamond, a urologist, both of Children's Hospital Boston, launched a formal monthly clinic to care for transgender children and adolescents. Both doctors were already seeing transgender patients, as well as children with all types of intersex conditions, but this clinic makes formal their commitment to the increasing numbers of kids who specifically identify as transgender. The monthly clinic, called GeMS (Gender Management Service), is the first such clinic in the US, and is promoted and supported by the hospital. In fact, articles in the "Children's News" publication of the hospital actively publicize the clinic. The hospital's website also promotes it as "the first major program in the United States that not only treats disorders of sexual differentiation [in children], but also works with transgendered children and young adults."

Children's Hospital Boston is a large, prestigious hospital in the middle of a district packed with medical facilities, just down the road from the Museum of Fine Arts. The hospital itself is a cheery place, as far as hospitals go, a modern structure with a bright, airy lobby, with children's artwork displayed on the walls and decorations in hues of purple, green, and blue.

The GeMS clinic, located on the 5th floor within the Endocrine Department, has no dedicated waiting area. Patients check in at the general waiting room, which noticeably has three restrooms—men's, women's, and a third one, gender-neutral. Clients are seen in several small examining rooms, where they might meet with the staff psychologist, Laura Edwards-Leeper, Spack, or Diamond. Spack's team also includes an endocrine nurse, a urology nurse, and other internists hoping to specialize in this burgeoning field.

Yet the kind of training needed to work with transgender patients is "not taught in medical school," according to Dr. Harvey Makadon, an associate professor at Harvard Medical School who is sitting in on the

Friday clinics. Dr. Spack agrees. "We are trained by our patients," he says, "and by experience." Luckily, he says, more medical students are now choosing to study specialties that are applicable in working with transgender kids.

During our visit, we are allowed to meet with a new patient, Jewel, whom Dr. Spack calls an "affirmed female," or transgirl. Jewel has just turned 17, and says she has known she is female since she was about 10, when she started dressing as a girl. Jewel has a small build, with long shiny black hair, piercing blue eyes, carefully applied makeup, and several facial piercings. She wears clothing typical for teenage girls, with layered tank tops and tight-fitting blue jeans, topped off with an ornamental belt and a small black purse.

Jewel has already been seeing a therapist for more than a year, and comes in with a letter from the therapist affirming Jewel's transgender status. Because her parents could not accept her identity as a trans teenager, Jewel now lives in a group home, and she has come to her appointment with a guardian. When Dr. Spack asks her what her dream is, Jewel is very clear that she would like to go on hormones as soon as possible and then have sex reassignment surgery in a year.

Dr. Spack visits with Jewel for quite a while. He advises her on her options, which can include taking the female hormone estrogen, which will quell the testosterone raging unbidden in her system. He explains that she will need the equivalent of four times the estrogen that biological females produce to knock down the amount of testosterone her 17-year-old body is producing and obtain the physical and emotional results she is seeking. He also explains that she will probably need to wait till she is at least 18 to find a surgeon willing to do sex reassignment surgery on her. In the meantime, he urges her to "be responsible" about her health— no smoking, and no street hormones. She nods her head gravely, with a shy smile.

Spack schedules another appointment for Jewel, with Laura, the staff psychologist. He tells her they will all decide together on the best course of her treatment. Jewel is feeling hopeful after the visit, and she and her guardian thank the doctor for his time. And now Jewel is one step closer to realizing her dream of finally becoming the woman she knows she is meant to be.

Resources

http://www.eje-online.org/cgi/content/full/155/suppl_1/S131
   Article from the Netherlands on treatments for transgender teens and possible side effects.

http://imatyfa.org/wp-content/uploads/2007/06/to-the-beat-of-a-different-drummer-6-2007.pdf
   Article in *Contemporary Pediatrics* (February 2005), by several doctors affiliated with the Gender Development Center at the Children's National Medical Center in Washington, DC. (Direct link to original article for physicians: http://www.modernmedicine.com/modern-medicine/article/articleDetail.jsp?id=147767)

http://www.wpath.org/
   Website of WPATH (World Professional Association for Transgender Health), formally the Harry Benjamin International Gender Dysphoria Association, Inc.

http://jcem.endojournals.org/cgi/reprint/88/8/3467.pdf
   Article in the *Journal of Clinical Endocrinology & Metabolism* (August 2003) on hormonal treatments and their side effects.

http://www.gires.org.uk/Web_Page_Assets/Hormonal_Medication.htm#Developing
   Information about the "Dutch protocol" and efforts of doctors to match these results.

Books

Transition and Beyond, Observations On Gender Identity, by Reid Vanderburgh (Q Press, 2007), available from the author or from bookstores.

*Transgender Emergence: Therapeutic Guidelines for Working With Gender-
Variant People and Their Families,* by Arlene Lev (Routledge, 2004).

Films

Just Call Me Kade, directed by Sam Zolten (2002), about a 16-year-old
transboy.

Transgeneration, directed by Jeremy Simmons (New Video Group, 2005),
a series about four transitioning college students.

Chapter 9

Legal Issues to Consider

WHEN YOUR CHILD is a minor it is up to you to secure their legal rights. It is important to stay aware of the rapidly changing laws pertaining to transgender people. This chapter provides an overview of the types of legal issues you and your transgender child may encounter. For more detailed information about the law in this area, or to talk with a lawyer about the specific issues involving your family, we have included a list of helpful websites and organizations in the resources at the end of this chapter.

Certain legal issues involving transgender children are of particular concern to parents and caregivers. The legality and logistics of changing a child's name on documents such as passports, birth certificates, and school forms is a major concern. Insurance coverage looms large once children begin transitioning; and custody problems with ex-partners and spouses can be common in families undergoing divorce or separation.

The field of transgender rights, for adults as well as children, is a rapidly developing area of law. Mostly, we see supportive laws and policies developing at the state and local level, but for that reason the laws and policies that affect you and your family will depend on where you live and what the issues are.

Most of the legal issues that transgender children encounter can be resolved through education. It's important to remember that most institutions are not familiar with transgender children and just may not know what procedures they should follow. By keeping up to date on the law in this area and advocating for your child when necessary, you not only make sure your child is treated fairly and respectfully, you also help ensure that our culture is more accepting of people of all gender identities. Please note: lawyers familiar with transgender law do not recommend arguing cases about transgender children in the courts at the present time.

Forms and Documentation

There are many occasions when you will need to identify the name and gender of your child on institutional or government documents. For many transgender people, including children, state-issued identification documents such as birth certificates and driver's licenses do not accurately reflect their name and gender.

In these situations parents of transgender children are faced with many questions: What name can I use when filling out paperwork for school registration? What if I need to show someone my child's birth certificate and it doesn't reflect their name or gender? Can my child get his or her name legally changed? While the answers to these questions will vary depending on the unique circumstance of your child, the following information can help you anticipate where your child may run into problems. You can find additional information on this topic on websites of legal organizations such as the Transgender Law Center. (Visit their website: http://www.transgenderlawcenter.org/)

Your Child's Legal Name

When a child is born, the name given on the birth certificate is their legal name. This name appears on all other state-issued identification documents, such as social security cards and Medicaid cards, and it is the name that is used for other legal documentation purposes, such as when registering for school or public benefits. As a parent, you can change the legal name of your child at any age. In most states, you need to go to court and get a court order; the process for doing this depends on where you live. Contact the court in your area or look for information on the Internet.

If you get a legal name change for your child, you can have all school records and other legal documentation changed to reflect his or her new name. This is a choice that some families make when the child is at a young age. Others simply call their child by a new name, but do not legally make any changes. This means the name their child goes by is different from the name on his or her birth certificate and other legal documents. Schools are not legally required to respect a child's name change unless it is legal. But as Shannon Price Minter of the National Center for Lesbian Rights, a specialist in transgender law, points out, "We have worked with many parents who have successfully advocated with their child's school to get the school to use their child's new name, even if the family has not gone through a legal name change. There are no laws that would prevent a school from calling transgender students by their chosen names, so most of the time all it takes is a little education to help a school understand that this is the right thing to do." We urge you to see what is possible in your own state or region and to advocate for your child regardless.

Social Security Cards

If you have your child's name changed legally, you can get the name on your child's social security card changed as well by filing a simple form. Information on how to do this is available on the SSA website. There is no gender marker on the social security card itself.

Gender Markers on Identification Documents

In most circumstances, state and public agencies look at a child's birth certificate to identify the child's gender for official purposes, such as granting public benefits, issuing a driver's license or state ID, or issuing a passport. If the gender marker on your child's birth certificate is different from the gender your child identifies as, it may be possible to change the gender marker on your child's birth certificate or work with public agencies to change the gender markers on the documents these agencies issue.

Birth Certificates

Almost every state allows transgender people to change the gender marker on their birth certificate after transitioning. While the process is different in each state, most states will not change a person's gender marker if they have not completed sex reassignment surgery. If your child has not had some form of gender-related surgery, it will be difficult, at this time, to change the gender marker on his or her birth certificate. In some states, the gender marker on a birth certificate can be changed if it was recorded incorrectly due to human error. This is sometimes called a "gender error."

If you are interested in changing the gender marker on your child's birth certificate, you should speak to a lawyer. In some instances a letter from your doctor indicating the error may suffice.

Please let us know if you are successful in changing your child's birth certificate, and if so, what approach you used, by contacting us at info@genderspectrum.org.

Passports

Transgender people can get the gender marker on their passport changed after completing some form of sex reassignment surgery. In general, it is difficult to get the gender marker changed on a transgender child's passport if he or she has not had gender-related surgery, unless you are leaving the country for the child to have this surgery. More information on the procedure for changing the gender marker on a passport can be found on the US Department of State's passport procedures website. If you are traveling out of the country with a transgender child, and the gender marker on the passport does not match your child's presentation, NCLR's Price Minter recommends that you carry a notarized doctor's letter with you explaining your child's medical situation. If your child has never had a passport before and your child's birth certificate has been changed to reflect their gender, it may not be a problem to get a passport reflecting your child's true gender without the proof of surgery.

Driver's Licenses and State Identification Cards

Most states have procedures for changing the name and gender on a driver's license or state ID. These laws vary on a state-by-state basis, so you need to check your state law. In some states, all that is needed is a legal name change order and a written letter or affidavit from a physician documenting that your child is in the process of gender transitioning. In most states, unless your child is an emancipated minor, the parents must fill out the necessary forms in support of their child.

Please let us know if you are successful in changing your child's driver's license or state ID card, and if so, what approach you used, by contacting us at info@genderspectrum.org.

Legal Issues in School

There are federal laws to support gender-variant and transgender students. There are also precedents set by states leading the way for transgender students, such as California.

All schools have a legal responsibility to treat all children respectfully and to maintain an environment where all students can get an education. This is true for transgender students too. If your child is being harassed or bullied by other students because of his or her gender, the school has a legal responsibility to respond to this harassment.

It's also important to note that schools *cannot* legally reveal medical information about any child, and there is *no* requirement that a letter informing other parents of your child's gender variance be sent out. Shannon Price Minter of the NCLR says, "School principals all over the country are finding that they can accommodate transgender children without any legal difficulties" for themselves or their schools as a result. Jenn Burleton, of TransActive Education & Advocacy, concurs. "The vast majority of school administrators do want to do the right thing." But it's up to parents, she suggests, to show them how the law can back up your requests. Schools, after all, don't want to be sued for noncompliance on this or any other front, she says.

Do not hesitate to advocate for your child—it is precisely your advocacy that will improve the situation for your child. If you do not know what to do, or are unclear about whether legal action is appropriate, refer to the legal resources at the end of this chapter for further advice. As legal procedures take a very long time, it is important to approach the school early on and let them know that you are aware of your child's legal rights and plan to take action if things are not immediately resolved. Just that action alone often causes a school to pause and examine the possible laws they may be violating by not supporting your child. If you are nervous about confronting the school on behalf of your child, find a friend or politically active community member to come with you.

Parents may also find that federally mandated special education programs, while not the right choice for every child, do offer more legal protections to students. See a lawyer knowledgeable about these issues in your state for more information.

The major issues for transgender and gender-variant schoolchildren are these:

- Names and pronouns
- Bathroom accessibility and comfort
- Gym/athletics

Please see Chapter 7, The Educational System and Your Family, for more information on the practical implications of these issues.

Navigating Gender-specific Activities, Forms, and Documents

If you have legally changed your child's name, it is easy to flash the court order to have their name changed on any form or registry. Sometimes that is all you need. If you are faced with a situation where a birth certificate is required, sometimes presenting documentation of a legal name change along with the birth certificate is all that is needed, and they will likely adjust the gender marker, as well. However, if you do not have documentation of a legal name change for your child, or if you want to be extra-prepared, it is helpful to obtain a note from your child's doctor. If the doctor says this is an issue of mistaken gender assignment and the child's true gender is different from the gender they present, any sports team or organization should honor it. Ask the doctor to state in the note that this is an issue of medical privacy and that this is confidential health information. Because of its confidentiality, organizations cannot legally share the information with anyone else. See Appendix 2 for a sample letter.

Team Sports

Prior to your child's puberty, with some determination, you should be able to secure your child a place on a youth sports team of their preferred gender. This can be done by conversing with coaches and league managers, providing a letter from a doctor or therapist, or showing some name-change documentation. If you are still experiencing discrimination, or are having problems registering your child to play sports, know that there are legal resources available to help you.

However, once your child enters puberty, it gets a little trickier, especially since male-bodied people are seen to have physical advantages. This should not be an issue in gym class—every child is entitled to participate in gym in accordance with their consistently presented gender. They are also entitled to an appropriate place to change for class. However, for competitive sports there are no clear-cut rules. The International Olympic Committee has recognized the existence of competitive transgender athletes and has developed a policy regarding the circumstances under which a transgender athlete can compete as their transitioned gender. In addition, the National Center for Lesbian Rights is working with a coalition of organizations to develop a similar policy for competitive athletics in secondary schools. But even without a written policy, many transgender youth are able to participate on sports teams as their identified gender.

> *My wrestling coach has allowed me on the team. He knows that I am trans, but he doesn't care. He is keeping it to himself.* —14-year-old transboy

> *My son needed a birth certificate to sign up for T-ball. Of course this says he is a female, so he was placed on a team for boys and girls, as a girl. I told the coach that my child is actually a little boy—he is a physical girl, but has gender dysphoria, or is transgender. The coach was great. No questions asked, my son became just another little boy playing T-ball. When we wanted to sign up for Cub Scouts, we were told that as long as the birth certificate said female, he was not allowed, so he will do swimming and martial arts instead.* —Parent of a 7-year-old transboy

> *We have a transgender girl on our cheerleading squad. She is great! We redesigned the tops so that they were not so revealing, and it wouldn't be so obvious that she didn't have any breasts. I thought it was weird, at first. But hey, I work in a high school, these things keep me young.* —High school coach

Custody Disputes and Divorce

It is important to remember that going to court to solve family disputes is not always the most effective approach for any family, and this is especially true for families with gender-variant or transgender children. Keep your family's situation in context: if your child lives in two households and you are experiencing disagreement about your child's gender expression and what is best for your child, obtain therapy and mediation as your first steps. Try to reach an understanding about how to proceed with your child. Keep in mind that it may be necessary to compromise, especially when your child is young. Once again, this outcome, though perhaps not ideal, is likely to be much preferable to going to court.

If your family is already in the family court system due to a contested custody situation or divorce and you are the parent of a gender-variant or transgender child, you should immediately seek the counsel of a lawyer familiar with transgender issues and rights. If you are concerned about how your child's other parent may present your parenting in relation to your child's gender expression, it is essential to be proactive and to cover your bases every step of the way.

It is advisable to secure professionals (doctors and therapists) to work with your family who could, if necessary, speak to the court about transgender issues and what they think is in the best interest of your child with respect to gender expression. These professionals should be able to work with all of your child's parents and help them to come to a mutual understanding of how to approach your child's parenting.

If you are in court, make sure your lawyer is very familiar with transgender issues. Family lawyers can contact organizations such as NCLR for consultation and assistance in locating local experts on transgender issues.

Parents have a constitutional right to parent as they see fit, as long as they are not physically or sexually abusing their children. When two legal parents disagree to such an extent that it is harmful to the child, or if their views cannot be reconciled, a judge must decide what should be done. The usual standard for judges' decisions is "the best interests of the child," but different states may have different standards.

We realize that this is only a starting point for the many legal issues you may find yourself confronting on behalf of your children. With attitudes and laws changing so rapidly, we can expect matters to get easier for transgender children and their families. We hope we have provided you with some specific tools and ideas about how best to proceed in your own communities. Remember, parents must advocate for the rights of their children, and blaze a trail for those who are following. You will not be alone in this; thousands of other parents across the country are doing similar work. And there are organizations and websites to assist or advise you. We wish you support in whatever struggles you encounter, and joy in whatever progress you are able to make.

Resources

Books

OutLaw: What LGBT Youth Should Know, by Lisa Keen (Beacon Press, 2007).

Transgender Rights, edited by Paisley Currah, Richard M. Juang, and Shannon Price Minter (University of Minnesota Press, 2006).

Organizations

National Center for Lesbian Rights: http://www.nclrights.org
Services are available to all, not only to lesbians. NCLR staunchly supports families with transgender family members.

Transgender Law Center: http://www.transgenderlawcenter.org/

Transgender Law and Policy Institute: http://www.transgenderlaw.org/

Sylvia Rivera Law Project: http://www.srlp.org/

Lambda Legal: http://www.lambdalegal.org/

National Center for Transgender Equality: http://www.nctequality.org/

National Gay and Lesbian Task Force: http://www.thetaskforce.org/

Gay and Lesbian Advocates & Defenders: http://www.glad.org/

For more regional organizations and organizations based outside the
US, visit http://www.transgenderlaw.org/links.htm.

Websites / Other Resources
Beyond the Binary: http://www.gsanetwork.org/BeyondtheBinary
/toolkit.html

GSA Network: http://www.gsanetwork.org/resources/FAQs.html

GLSEN: http://www.glsen.org/cgi-bin/iowa/all/home/index.html

Conclusion

IT IS A VERY EXCITING TIME to be raising gender-variant and transgender children. For the very first time, people want to understand and learn more about these children. Just by reading this book, you are on your way to a better understanding of what you can do as a parent, educator, or care provider to help that person in your life who inspired you to learn more about this subject. Congratulations. You are helping to change the world.

When a significantly gender-variant or transgender child or teen has touched your life, you come to understand very quickly that it is your beliefs that must change, not this child. It is these children who are inspiring this movement. And it is their loving parents who are leading the social change.

It takes a particularly brave and courageous child to continue to assert their truth, a truth that runs counter to the mainstream. These gender-variant and transgender children—often intelligent, artistic, and sensitive kids—are doing just that. Their inner integrity guides them. They struggle over and over again to show the world who they are. All they ask is to be themselves.

As we hope you realize by now, parents have an amazing ability to positively influence the lives of these children, each and every day. Likewise, educators, doctors, therapists, and all others who work with children share the responsibility to understand and respectfully interact with the next generation of children with greater awareness and sensitivity to gender diversity.

Parents can give these cross-gender and gender-variant children the room to be exactly who they are. Give them love, support, compassion and encouragement, teach them that they deserve to live, show them that they matter by sticking up for them, and demonstrate support by actively combating gender discrimination. Never underestimate what love can do. Use your love as parents to inspire you to take action. It does not matter on what scale you work. By being proud of your child and honoring who they are without embarrassment or shame, you are changing the world. As you nurture and nourish their brave spirits, you nurture and nourish a more diverse future.

There is a learning curve here, of course. Growth is always accompanied by growing pains. It is also the pathway to expanded perspectives and deeper levels of satisfaction in life. We all want to keep our minds and hearts flexible as we age and grow. As adults we must unlearn what we thought we knew to be true in order to embrace a new and fuller truth. And there is nothing like a gender-variant or transgender child or teen to shake up any rigid beliefs you once held!

So even after reading this book, there may be things you don't know, fears you still have, and issues you have yet to confront. However, with education, encouragement, the right tools, and a community of support, you will be up to the task.

We urge you to continue working for gender equity and gender diversity and the rights of your child. Join with other parents and work for the legal, social, and educational rights of your children. Support them in their self-expression and watch as they grow and thrive.

We hope you have found this book helpful. We have written it with you and your family in mind. We have also written it so that professionals will have more information and empathy for the needs of gender-variant and transgender children and their families. Let us know what you found most helpful, and what you might like to see in a future edition, by contacting us through Gender Spectrum at www.genderspectrum.org.

This book is dedicated to the transgender and gender-variant children and teens of today, who are insisting that we rise to the occasion. It is also dedicated to those of you who love and support them. Our hats are off to all of you.

Remember, we truly can—and will—change the world!

Stephanie Brill
Rachel Pepper

Who Will Be Role Models for Our Children?

Despite the fact that many transgender people have lived very privately, we do know they have always existed. If you are looking for role models for your children, here are a few contemporary folks to consider.

Joan Roughgarden: Biologist and author of *Evolution's Rainbow.* http://www.stanford.edu/group/roughlab/rough.html

Lucas Silveira: Lead singer of the Toronto-based band The Cliks. http://www.myspace.com/thecliks

Dragonsani "Drago" Renteria: Founder of the national Deaf Queer Resource Center. http://www.deafqueer.org/

Georgina Beyer: The world's first openly transgender Member of Parliament, representing the Labour Party in New Zealand from 1999 to 2007. http://www.georginabeyer.com/

Shannon Price Minter: Lawyer for the National Center for Lesbian Rights, specializing in transgender legal issues. http://www.nclrights.org/

Katastrophe: San Francisco–based rapper.
http://www.katastropherap.com/

Hiromasa Ando: Japanese speedboat racer.
http://www.ftmaustralia.org/library/02/hiromasa.html

Imani Henry: Activist and performance artist. http://www.geocities.com /imani_henry/

Kate Bornstein: Author, playwright, performance artist, and gender theorist. http://www.tootallblondes.com/KatePages/kate_bornstein.htm

For more, visit http://en.wikipedia.org/wiki/List_of_transgender_people.

Sample Doctor's Letters

The two letters below are examples of letters your doctor can write in support of your child. Your doctor may modify them to reflect your child's circumstances. The first letter is a document we advise you to have your child carry at all times. You can present the second letter in support of allowing your transgender child to play in competitive sports. Thank you to Dr. Nick Gorton for his kind permission to use these letters.

Letter 1

To whom it may concern,

I am a physician licensed to practice medicine and surgery in the state of California. I have personally evaluated John Doe.

John is a transgender boy. He has been diagnosed with Gender Identity Disorder of Childhood (302.6). Part of the treatment in youth with severe GID, as John has, involves allowing them to live in the gender role appropriate to their true psychological gender, which in John's case is male. Eventually many children with GID require hormonal and surgical treatment after entering adolescence. However, in preadolescent patients treatment is generally restricted to social and psychological treatment.

It is imperative to the health and well-being of children with this complex medical condition that they be allowed to live life fully in the appropriate gender role. In John's case this requires that he be allowed to participate in appropriate activities, as any boy his age would.

When children are gender-segregated for any reason or activity, it is crucial that John be allowed to participate with boys his own age. Sex-segregating him with girls could potentially cause irreparable psychological damage. John should be allowed to use the boy's bathroom, locker room, and any other sex-segregated facility for children.

It is also imperative that John's confidentiality be protected. Revealing his transgender status is not only potentially psychologically damaging, it would compromise the confidentiality of his private medical history.

Thank you in advance for your help in providing John a supportive and healthy environment. If you have any questions or concerns, please do not hesitate to contact me either at my office or, if urgent, at my cell phone number: xxx-xxx-xxxx.

Sincerely,
Name of Doctor here

Letter 2

To whom it may concern,

I am a physician licensed to practice medicine and surgery in the state of California. I have personally evaluated John Doe. John is a transgender boy and has been diagnosed with Gender Identity Disorder of Childhood (302.6). As part of his treatment, he has been living in the male role full-time for many years. John now desires to participate in youth athletics. It is medically appropriate that he participate as a male athlete.

The question of athletic participation has been addressed at a number of different levels in sport, including a statement by the International Olympic Committee that allows adult transgender athletes to participate according to their gender identity. The IOC also expects adult athletes to have a hormonal milieu that is appropriate for the gender in which they participate. For example, an adult female-to-male transgender athlete would be expected to take supplemental testosterone so that his testosterone level would be in the normal male range. This is because much of the difference in performance between male and female athletes is due to the effect of hormones on the musculoskeletal system.

In preadolescent children such as John, the hormonal milieu does not differ significantly between the sexes, so that any hormonally based advantage or disadvantage is unimportant. While sex segregation in sport does happen with preadolescent children, it is a purely social segregation rather than being based on any significant physiological difference.

By participating in youth athletics, John will not be at any greater or lesser risk of injury and will have no advantage or disadvantage compared with other, nontransgender, boys his age. However, denying John the opportunity to participate in age- and gender-appropriate activities with boys his age is potentially significantly psychologically damaging. Living fully in the new gender role is an important part of treatment for transgender patients, and being denied participation can cause psychological trauma—which I would expect to be significantly more damaging for a child than an adult. Therefore, I strongly recommend that John be allowed to participate in boys' soccer.

In addition, it is imperative that John's confidentiality be protected. Revealing his transgender status would not only be profoundly damaging, but would also reveal his confidential medical history.

If you have any questions or concerns, please do not hesitate to contact me.

Sincerely,
Name of Doctor here

About the Authors

STEPHANIE BRILL has provided education and support to countless families with gender-nonconforming children across the United States and Canada. She has conducted in-depth training about gender identity development and gender expression in children to doctors, social workers, therapists, and educators since 2002. To give this important teaching and training work a national reach, she cofounded Gender Spectrum Education and Training in 2007. Stephanie cofounded and facilitates the support group at Children's Hospital Oakland for parents of gender-variant and transgender children, and she coproduces the yearly Gender Spectrum Family Conference in Seattle. Stephanie is also a midwife and the author of two other books: *The Queer Parents' Primer* and *The New Essential Guide to Lesbian Conception, Pregnancy and Birth.*

Stephanie would like to honor two of her personal inspirations—Shannon Price Minter and Caitlin Ryan—for the amazing work they are doing. She extends heartfelt appreciation to each and every family of gender-variant and transgender children for leading the way to a brand-new world. She appreciates all the educators and health care professionals who are taking the time to educate themselves about how to best serve these brave children and their families. A special thanks goes out to Park Day School for its willingness to blaze a trail, and to Dr. Herbert Schreier for cofounding the Oakland Support Group with her. Endless gratitude to Aidan Key for his desire to join paths. Thanks to

Cleis Press for being ready to publish this book, and to Rachel Pepper for an unexpected collaboration. Thanks also to Wendy Brill for her insightful feedback. Most of all, Stephanie would like to thank her radiant partner, Kristin, and the four amazing children they love so unconditionally. This book would never have come into being without them.

RACHEL PEPPER is currently Coordinator of LGBT Studies at Yale University. She is coauthor of the Princeton Review's *Gay and Lesbian Guide to College Life* (Princeton Review, 2007) and author of the *Ultimate Guide to Pregnancy for Lesbians* (Cleis Press, second edition, 2005). She contributes to many magazines and newspapers and is the long-standing book editor for Curve Magazine. Rachel has found it an honor to work on this groundbreaking book. She would like to thank all the parents who completed the lengthy questionnaire that helped in her research and provided so many of the quotes included in this book's pages. Thanks also to the Park Day School, the NCLR, Dr. Norman Spack, Cleis Press, Jessica Pettit for her suggestions on the college material, and copyeditor Mark Rhynsburger. Much appreciation is due to Yale University's Office of the Provost for research funds enabling the author to attend the Gender Spectrum Family Conference in Seattle. Rachel especially thanks her daughter, Frances Ariel, for her patience during many research and writing hours, and for inspiring her to learn, love, and laugh each and every day. And finally, thanks to Stephanie for agreeing to this collaboration and helping turn a book dream into reality.